# Dear Mother

To John and Mary Bosanko
and Patrick Love
whose help has been unstinting.

# Dear Mother

## GREAT WAR LETTERS FROM A BRISTOL SOLDIER

> have been issued to me: keep them carefully
> please as I may want them sooner or
> later.
> Now, mother, please be cheerful while I am
> away because after all it is only right
> that I should go; and many and many
> others have gone to do more than I.
> it is the right place for all Englishmen
> now and we are only taking a small part
> in a great work. If God wills, I shall
> come back to you safe and sound; if I
> do not, why there is nothing hard in
> dying for a great cause; after all it
> is the cause that matters and not the life
> of this individual or that. I trust God
> will give me courage, patience and endurance
> in danger and hardship and I hope only
> to do my duty as an English gentleman
> and these things are greater and worthier

Edited by

## BARRY WILLIAMSON

First published on 11th November 2003 by Redcliffe Press Ltd.,
81g Pembroke Road, Bristol BS8 3EA

© Barry Williamson and Bristol Grammar School

ISBN 1 904537 07 3

British Cataloguing-in-Publication Data.
A catalogue record for this book is available from the British Library.

Designed and typeset by Stephen Morris, smc@freeuk.com
Printed by HSW, Tonypandy, South Wales

# CONTENTS

page

7 Key Dates in the Life of Stanley Booker

9 Preface

11 SCHOOL DAYS AND OXFORD

21 JOINING UP: NO 14605

26 TRAINING WITH THE WORCESTERSHIRE REGIMENT

53 FROM BISLEY TO BRENTWOOD

85 SALISBURY PLAIN AT LAST

99 AT THE FRONT

126 KILLED IN ACTION

131 TRACKING DOWN THE BOOKERS

134 List of illustrations and maps

136 Notes

142 Acknowledgements

# KEY DATES IN THE LIFE OF STANLEY BOOKER

| | |
|---|---|
| 17 January 1893 | Born at 41 Pembroke Road, Bristol |
| September 1903 | Entered Bristol Grammar School |
| 24 March 1908 | Confirmed by Bishop Marsden at St Bartholomew's Church, Bristol |
| October 1912 | At St John's College, Oxford, having won an open scholarship in classics |
| 4 August 1914 | Britain declared war on Germany |
| 24 September 1914 | Enlisted in the 12th Battalion, the Gloucestershire Regiment |
| 29 March 1915 | Commissioned in the Worcestershire Regiment |
| April 1915 | Began training at Maldon, Essex |
| September 1915 | More training at Bisley, Epping and Brentwood |
| February 1916 | On Salisbury Plain |
| 23 May 1916 | Left Southampton on ss *Caesarea* for Le Havre |
| 1 June 1916 | In trenches at Richebourg-Saint-Vaast |
| 21 July 1916 | Rescued wounded men leading to the award of the M C |
| 10/11 October 1916 | Killed at Richebourg-L'Avoue |

Opposite: SCB wearing the uniform of a Lieutenant in
The Worcestershire Regiment, taken in the
spring of 1916 when he returned home on leave

# PREFACE

If you climb the stairs to the Great Hall in Bristol Grammar School you will see in front of you, behind the Headmaster's table, the memorial to those boys who died in the Great War. There are 121 names in all. Almost none of them has any personal meaning for present-day pupils who daily attend assembly and eat lunch in the Hall.

In March 2001 a class of Year 9 pupils took one name at random from the long list – Stanley Charles Booker. They were studying the Great War as part of the History syllabus and I was concerned that my explanation of the causes, course and consequences gave the subject a remote anonymity. I wanted them to see the war through the experience of one individual and to explore what his death meant for his family.

It was fairly easy to collect a wallet of raw material on Stanley Booker from the School archives (magazine entries and team photographs), the City Library (street directories and newspaper obituaries) and the Worcestershire Regiment in whose 2/7th Battalion Stanley was serving when he died. Unfortunately, St John's College Oxford could not produce anything other than brief biographical details and the Public Record Office said that all his War Office papers were destroyed in bombing raids during the last war although we later discovered that this was not the case. However, pupils became immersed in the job of researching and writing History and they all produced a biography of Stanley Booker. I think they enjoyed the process.

There the exercise might have ended but for the persistence of several pupils who insisted that we must search for any Booker relatives in Bristol in the hope that they might possess family papers. I reluctantly agreed, explaining that few families kept such papers after the first generation and we were unlikely to succeed. I was wrong and this book is the result.

Brothers: Walter, Harold and SCB

# SCHOOL DAYS AND OXFORD

Stanley Charles Booker was born on 17th January 1893 at 41 Pembroke Road, Clifton, Bristol, the second son of James and Sarah Booker. The family was living in rooms they had probably rented from a Miss Cook who ran the Victoria School of Music in the house. Some months later they moved to a newly built house at 64 Chesterfield Road, St Andrew's Park and there the family remained until the early 1940s. There were three brothers, Harold, Stanley and Walter and a cousin remembers that they were a 'God-fearing and hospitable' family. They were also a family who preserved carefully everything that might be of interest to later generations. Stanley's brother Walter became a clergyman and left a draft of every sermon he ever preached, daily account books and a box of Stanley's wartime papers lovingly collected by their mother. The father, James Thomas Booker, came originally from Cheltenham and was a master grocer with a shop in Boyce's Avenue in Clifton. He retired about 1913.

Stanley went first to Miss Bartlett's school at 49 Belvoir Road and then in 1903 to Bristol Grammar School, which his two brothers Harold and Walter also attended. Fees were £12 a year. When he arrived at the school its fortunes were at a low ebb. Robert Leighton had been Headmaster for 20 years and his energy had waned. The school was almost bankrupt, there were fewer than 200 boys and they had a reputation for ill-disciplined behaviour in the streets. On Tuesday afternoons the boys attended school but the masters declined to do so; the Sergeant organised mass singing and drawing 'lessons' in the Great Hall.

Stanley was lucky that the new Headmaster in 1906 was Cyril Norwood[1], one of the great schoolmasters of the early twentieth century and later Headmaster of Marlborough and Harrow. He set up a new House system, reformed the punishment system which was strictly enforced and began a building programme which provided new classrooms, fives courts, a gymnasium and cricket pavilion. He also wrote the school song. It was soon obvious that Booker, SC was a star pupil. He regularly won form prizes, became a lance-

41 Pembroke Road
Clifton, Bristol where
SCB was born

Boyce's Avenue, Clifton, about 1913. James Booker's grocer's shop was on the right, next to the corner shop

corporal in the Cadet Corps and played in the 1st XV Rugby team in 1910 and 1911: 'a hard-working forward who always does his best, scrums well but might be better in the loose,' reported the 1910 *Chronicle*. He was a school prefect in 1911 and Secretary of the Debating Society, speaking in 1912 against the motion 'That the erection of a statue to King Edward VII before the Victoria Rooms serves no useful purpose' and against the motion that 'England is a degenerate nation'.

The Headmaster took a particular interest in the Cadet Corps and provided a new rifle range on the school field. In 1911 the *Chronicle* carried a report of a Corps exercise led by the Headmaster, Capt Norwood. It was almost surrealist in its foretaste of things to come. The cadets left Redland Station by special train at 1.15pm and reached Kelston, a village between Bristol and Bath at 2pm. The 'enemy' travelled on the same train and alighted at Bitton. The objective was to engage and repulse the enemy at North Stoke. The Headmaster led one contingent and 'about 3.30 our scouts brought in news

Dr Cyril Norwood
during his time as
Headmaster of Bristol
Grammar School

The Great Hall at the school when it was still used for teaching before 1914

The school 1st XV in 1911 with SCB on the left of the middle row. By 1918 they had won five M.C.s and one V.C. and five of the team were dead

that the enemy had been seen not far off.' The enemy advanced but the defenders held onto the racecourse at Lansdown. A cease-fire sounded at 4pm and the train was waiting at Kelston for the return to Redland in time for tea. Would that such exercises were always to be so painless. The reporter for the magazine wrote with cheerful optimism, 'It was quite a novel experience to get into the firing line.'

1912 saw Booker at the peak of his school reputation. On 16th March he came third in the three-mile race with a time of 18 minutes 21 seconds and at the prize giving in July he won six major school prizes and the Bristol Scholarship to St John's College Oxford where he had already won an Open Scholarship in Classics at the age of 17. There seemed to be nothing he could not achieve when he went up to Oxford in October 1912.

Very few letters from Stanley to his mother survive from Oxford and the first is postmarked 26th January 1913:

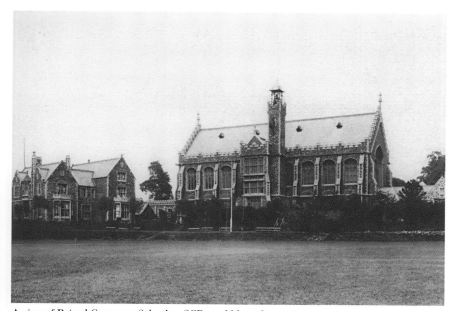

A view of Bristol Grammar School as SCB would have known it

SCB in 1912
before he left for
St John's College,
Oxford

St John's College
Oxford

Dear Mother
You will find enclosed a copy of my battels[2] which I received last Monday
and have to pay tomorrow. I did not send them down when I got them as
I had told you what I expected them to be and as you will see they are
rather less.

I will send tomorrow also a cheque to Mr Woolway and another to Mr
Holborn and then it will be quite alright and I shall be out of debt.

I have spent of my own money 2/2$d$ since last Sunday and a penny I have
lost. My weekly battels are 19/4$d$. I shall have on Wednesday week to give
a breakfast to the crews of the boats rowing in the Torpids. I have joined
two other 'freshers' in doing so and it will cost I suppose 25/- or so each.
It is one of the University and College customs that men in their first year
entertain the boat crews. At St John's as there are two boats there are 16
men to start with then 4 spare men and probably a couple of coaches so
that with the hosts the breakfast party will be 25 or so. The breakfast will
be in Hall and I daresay I shall have to preside. The rowing men are to

go into training tonight. They must get to bed no earlier that 10 o'clock and no later than 10.30: they must be up at 7: have porridge in the kitchen at 7.10: run round the Gardens once and walk round twice: then have breakfast in Hall at 8.30: practically no lunch: no smoking and no eating between meals. In the afternoon of course they row and they have to eat a full dinner of 5 courses and they are advised to take two glasses of port after it. They must eat as much as they can to increase their strength and take exercise to keep down the fat.

I received the shield quite safely: thank you very much for it. I am afraid I have been costing you a lot in regard to postage but I hope I shall not want very much more. The shield is now hanging up and on my light paper looks very effective. I only hope the Head will be up: I should like to see him very much, of course if he came I could not fail to see him as he would dine in our Hall. With the calendar Maud sent me all I want now is one picture on one wall and a very small photo or something on the other. I shall get them as they could hardly cost more than 2/-.

I have had no extraordinary happenings this week: I have had two games of hockey and no football. I have been to tea with Mr & Mrs Ball[3] today and on Friday I was with another scholar. Webb came up on Monday and Edwards and he had tea with me on Tuesday and we had a very enjoyable time together. Webb will not be able to play any games for a month at least and still feels a few twinges of rheumatism. All that he has left to do is to go out walking and perhaps I shall be able to join him sometimes. I saw him again yesterday afternoon.

I shall have to stay up a few days at the end of the term. I have to take the examination in Holy Scripture which starts on the last Wednesday of term and the 'viva voce' exams occur from Tuesday to Wednesday. There are three sets of examiners who take fellows according to their first letter of their names: as I am a B I suppose I shall get it over on Tuesday before the examiners who take from A to G. At any rate it will be over by Wednesday. It will be cheaper to stay up than to come down and come up especially for the exam ...

Thank Harold and Walter for their letters and give my love to father, aunt and them, my love to you and best wishes in all things but above all don't worry for me.
Your loving son
Stanley.

The next letter is marked 'Private' and dated 16th February 1913:

St John's College
Oxford

Dear Mother

I am writing to you like this because I want to tell you this first and then you may let the rest know as much as you think right. Along with your letter which came on Friday I received a letter from Irene telling me that we could no longer correspond. The reason was this. She said as I knew she and Cox had been friends from infancy and up to quite lately had always regarded him as such. Now she said something had occurred to make her think of another relationship (those were her own words). So you see I have been abruptly dismissed. I wrote and said that I was quite content and posted the letter that evening. Later she sent me another letter that night which told me she was sorry to send such a letter on St Valentine's day and that she and Cox had been meeting each other lately. This morning I received a letter from Mrs Cuttle asking me to say nothing if I hear of anything more than friendship between Irene and anyone. Mrs Cuttle says she has made up her mind and so has Irene that Irene must be free until she knows her own mind which she certainly does not at present.

I have replied that I will do of course as she says. So you see it apparently comes to this: while I have been away Cox has stepped in and taken her from me and they are now engaged and her people do not like it. I have written to Cox to tell him I do not consider him a friend anymore.

I have told Edwards because he corresponds with the Coxes and knows how affairs have been with me. This I did so that he should not do or say anything which might make matters worse or create any awkwardness. Edwards is a good friend to me and when we are down again he must certainly come up to our place so that you can know him better.

I need not say this news has upset me very much: when I come down again I shall have only you at home and Leslie, Wilfred and my other school friends to think of who I know will be true to me. Please give Aunt my love and tell her that now I am away I realise how good she has been and is to me.

Please accept my love for yourself which is now more than I can ever tell you. I often think of you and wonder whether I ought to be here while you are at home slaving hard when the time has come when you should look to us to support the home. However, you must be sure that I will do nothing if I can help it to make things worse and in time to come I will try and do something to repay you for all your anxiety and labour for me. I shall be glad to be with you again although you must not think I will not like Oxford life. I do like it though I always long to see my mother and family again.

Please give my love to father and tell him I hope he is well in every way and that I shall be very glad to see him again. Give him my best wishes and I am going to write him a letter this week.

The other news you will find in my other letters: but you will understand why I have thus written to you alone in this matter. Forgive me if I have caused you any anxiety over it more than you already have: believe me mother I am
Your loving son
Stanley.


In early June he received a letter from his old Headmaster:

My Dear Booker
Yes, I saw that you did not get a mention in the Gaisford[4] but I did not think it was quite your vein ...

I did not know that you had been ill and hope that Oxford at its best as it must now be, will set you up again. It is worthwhile to have a look at the country all round Oxford, for it is fine of its type and most Oxford men are shut up too much in the limits of the place.

The late nineties were evil days and the college did not pull together. As to the school, Mr Beames did well to whet your curiosity and I shall not dull its edge. With Mr Asquith, wait and see: you will not have to wait long. Room 1 where you used to pursue the various muses is now a ruin, an unsightly heap of tumbled bricks and mortar...

On the other side however the science wing rises in shapely fashion and dwarfs the pavilion ...

Today the second XI won a glorious victory over the children of the Cathedral School.

You must forgive a short letter as this is my 19th today. See to it that you get fit, even at the temporary cost of your work, for Oxford is the worst of places to be run down in ...
Yours very truly
Cyril Norwood

Thus passed Stanley's first year at Oxford. From his second year there are no surviving letters. Surprisingly, he failed to gain the expected First in Classical Moderations at the end of his second year. However, any anxiety over such mundane matters was soon overtaken by events in Europe.

64 Chesterfield Road, St Andrews Park where the Bookers lived from 1894 to the early 1940s

On Tuesday 4th August 1914 Britain declared war on Germany. Stanley was at home in Bristol for the Long Vacation. His course at Oxford had two more years to run but he immediately wanted to volunteer for the army. As a member of the Oxford University Officers' Training Corps he was in line for a commission. His only anxiety was that his scholarship at St John's would not be kept open for him when he returned from the War so he wrote to the President of the College: 'I would like to know whether the College would receive me back if safe and well at the conclusion of peace and allow me the full enjoyment of the scholarship I now hold for it is scarcely possible war will be ended before the beginning of next term...' The College replied on 8th August that they would keep his scholarship open till he returned because 'that was the arrangement made by all colleges during the Boer War... and no one should suffer in his academic course for doing his duty to his country.' In any case, Stanley expected to be back at Oxford by Christmas.

Meanwhile in Bristol there was a rush to enlist. Kitchener, the new Secretary of State for War, appealed for volunteers and local recruiting committees were formed to administer the process. They had to be responsible for clothing, accommodation and food until the Army was ready to accept the men. The Bristol Committee, chaired by the Lord Mayor[1] decided to recruit a Citizens' Battalion for the Gloucestershire Regiment which would consist of young men from 'the Mercantile and Professional Classes'. The battalion was to be known as Bristol's Own. Recruiting opened at the Colston Hall on 15th August and was supervised by two retired officers – Col WEP Burgess and Capt WAR Blennerhasset[2]. On 1st October recruiting closed for this battalion as 990 men and 31 officers had enlisted. Over 100 Old Boys of Bristol Grammar School joined up in the same battalion so Stanley would have been amongst many friends.

His papers in the War Office service files indicate the process of enlistment. There was the completion of a Short Service Attestation Form, No. B2065, a medical examination and then the swearing of an oath of obedience in the presence of a magistrate or an officer. Stanley enlisted on 24th September but his medical form is dated three days earlier. This may be due to the discovery of his weak eyesight which was so bad that he could not read the third line of the chart and it would have been impossible for him to see an enemy soldier in the trenches across No Man's Land. Perhaps the recruiting officer indicated quietly that he should go out and buy glasses and return a few days later with satisfactory sight, wearing glasses. Dr Dobyn then signed the declaration: 'He can see the required distance with either eye: his heart and lungs are healthy: he has the free use of his joints and limbs and he declares that he is not subject to fits of any description.' On the date of signing Stanley was 21 years 9 months old, 5 feet 8 inches tall and weighed 140lbs. The medical examination also required the measuring of 'chest fully expanded'; it was 38 inches. His complexion was dark, his eyes brown and hair black. The final stage was the swearing of the oath: 'I will be faithful and bear true Allegiance to His Majesty King George the Fifth, His Heirs and Successors … and will observe and obey all orders of His Majesty, His Heirs and Successors and of the Generals and Officers set over me. So help me God.'

Recruiting at the Colston Hall, Bristol, precise date unknown. The men leaving the building had presumably just signed on

The Tudor buildings at the Ashton Gate exhibition ground when it was open to the public from late June to mid-August 1914. These were later used as HQ buildings for the Bristol battalion

Recruits carrying their bedding into the Dominions Pavilion at the International Exhibition in late October 1914. One of the Wills tobacco bonded warehouses is in the background

D Company having a meal in their barracks at Ashton Gate, Bristol. SCB was a member of this company

Bristol's Own drilling at Ashton Gate before the arrival of uniforms although they are carrying rifles

Digging trenches at Ashton Gate in the autumn of 1914. This activity kept a good number of men occupied without requiring much equipment

A church parade passing along North Street, probably in the spring of 1915

It must have been a great disappointment to Stanley that he was not selected for a commission as an officer as would have been normal with someone who had served so successfully in his school and university training corps. The reason was his defective eyesight.

Having completed the recruitment of this battalion of 1,021 men the local committee had to decide on accommodation and training. Nothing was ready so the recruits lived at home until mid-October on a two shillings a day allowance plus the soldiers' daily shilling. They reported each morning for drill at the Artillery Ground in Whiteladies Road. There were no rifles or uniforms available and therefore recruits wore a small circular badge on their left lapel to indicate they had enlisted. Eventually a camp was made for the battalion in the Exhibition Ground at Ashton Gate, known as White City[3]; the buildings had been erected for an international exhibition and the pavilions were simply adapted as barracks and the mock Tudor village was HQ. The committee eventually purchased uniforms and boots but the 200 cases of Boer War rifles they hoped to use had all rusted, so they borrowed a number from Horfield barracks. Most of the training therefore had to be marching, digging trenches and athletic competitions.

In February 1915 Stanley was promoted to lance corporal, a sign that his qualities were being recognised despite his defective eyesight. He applied for a commission later that month, went before a selection board chaired by Brigadier General Sir Hugh Stewart Bt.[4] and by a process we cannot now discover, was appointed as 2nd Lieutenant in the 2/7th Battalion of the Worcestershire Regiment on 29th March 1915. The probability is that the Worcesters were short of officers, their commanding officer knew the 12th Gloucesters were a likely source and contact was made. Stanley had to produce a Certificate of Moral Character signed by the Vicar of St Bartholomew's, his home church, and he himself signed the General Service Agreement whereby he promised to serve in any place outside the United Kingdom 'in the event of national emergency.' It was to be another 14 months before he set foot in France.

# TRAINING WITH THE WORCESTERSHIRE REGIMENT

In 1915 the 2/7th Worcesters were one of four infantry battalions each of about 30 officers and 970 men, making up the 183rd Brigade which was one of three brigades forming the 61st Division (12,000 men). As a Second Lieutenant, Stanley was in charge of a platoon of about 50 men which formed part of 'A' Company. There were four platoons in each company which was commanded by a captain. Stanley was sometimes put in charge of the whole company, as in August 1915, when Capt Boucher and Lt Butcher went on leave. He appeared to relish the challenge and explained to his mother that the company commander 'has to be father, mother and every relation to his men... if they are in any trouble whatsoever he has to see to it.'

At Easter 1915, at about the time that Stanley joined them, the 61st Division moved from Northampton to Chelmsford in Essex where it acted as a holding and drafting unit supplying replacements for casualties suffered by the 48th Division in France. The 61st had a poor reputation based mainly on the fact that it was always understrength, was forced to train with defective equipment (the issue of modern .303 SMLE rifles was delayed until two months before embarkation for France) and it frequently lost senior officers to other divisions.

Stanley's earliest surviving letter from his war service was sent to his mother from Maldon on 25th April 1915. He appears to have been a regular Sunday letter writer even when he was at the front. The letters are substantial, usually seven or eight quarto pages long and he always apologised to his mother if he had missed a week through pre-occupation with military duties. There are 51 letters in this collection from the war years, all written to his mother except three to his old headmaster, Dr Norwood. Stanley began writing to his mother when he left Bristol in April 1915 and continued until the month he was killed, October 1916. Some letters must have been lost but we do not know how many. The word total is about 75,000 and has been reduced here by about one third. The letters present few problems of comprehension; the handwriting is clear, the spelling is faultless, the punctuation is interesting and the paragraphs are coherent. In only one respect is there a problem: none of the letters is dated except three from training and three from the front. However, many are still in their postmarked envelopes and for others there are sometimes internal clues such as a brother's birthday or a Zeppelin raid. Each letter begins 'Dear Mother', and ends with the same long coda of good wishes and love to friends and family. The latter has been omitted after the first two. How far Stanley self-censored the news so as to protect his family we can only guess. He certainly worried that they were worried about him. The letters are perhaps surprising in that there is a total absence of cynicism or self-pity. They are the letters of an ordinary soldier, sometimes weary of training and of waiting to be sent to the front. But they are untouched by the mood of despair and futility that followed the carnage on the Somme. Stanley knew why he should join up and fight for his country. It was simply to do his duty to stop Germany bullying the small countries of Europe and getting away with uncivilised behaviour. He explained this in a letter home on 1st August 1915:

'Well mother, you ought to be glad you are able to give your sons and if German mothers can lose their sons simply to make Germany dominant in Europe we ought to be able to do more to end all the old barbarous ideas Germany stands for and to make it plain the strong shall no longer override the weak'; and in another letter, 'It is better to be serving than to win all the prizes in Oxford.'

c/o Mr Stebbing
Heybridge Hall[1]
Maldon
Essex
[Postmarked 25th April 1915]

Dear Mother
This week has been free from alarms and I have had a comparatively quiet time. Monday was the same as usual with ordinary parades:

Tuesday we went out, carried out a very interesting attack practice which entailed crossing a river over a bridge on which a machine gun was supposed to be trained, and in which I met Lt Col Hird, chief of our Divisional Staff and a charming man at that. That night I had to take charge of the picquet and was on 24 hrs duty from 6pm to 6pm. Wednesday was unutterably boring, and I spent it in feeling tired and sleepy after being up at night: Thursday saw more attack practice, while Friday I was on the range at Woodham Mortimer and Saturday I did the same.

That's the week's programme: Tuesday's was at once the most interesting and the most boring duty of the whole. The picquet consisted of 30 men, 1 sgt, 2 corporals and 2 lance-corporals: and it was meant for any emergencies. At the top of the street where Headquarters are is a church, disused because unsafe with a square tower[2]: it is one of the highest points in Maldon and a good view all the way round can be obtained from it: here we had two sentries, one at the top and one at the bottom. The picquet was stationed at Headquarters and I had to take the Adjutant's room to sleep in and be ready for emergencies: one of my chief duties was to mount the tower and keep a look out for suspicious lights and if I saw any I was to report them to the Quarter Master. If anything did happen I was to send at once for the Colonel and Adjutant. We were given ammunition to

Heybridge Hall near Maldon where SCB was billeted from April to August 1915

use in case of anything. However nothing happened. I went up the tower three times during the night: the first time about 8.30, I most distinctly did see some signalling by means of lights but I do not know what they were or how far off they were. They stopped in about 5 minutes so that we could take no action. Next time I went up about 11.30 and all was clear but at 12.30 I went up again and watched for an hour myself. This time I saw a light come up and flicker, send up clouds of smoke and die away to a faint glow then flicker up again and so continue: with all the smoke I thought it was a fire breaking out and sent for the police: we managed to drag a round, fat, heavy gasping Special Constable up the stairs and showed it to him. He took a little time to discover his direction and then he told us it was the Gasworks and they were 'drawing the retorts' whatever that may be. So my one alarm was groundless. I got to sleep about 2.45am but I kept waking with the cold.

Next morning I was very sleepy but I went up on the tower several times and had a good look round. I could see down the Blackwater, almost to the sea. There is a bend which prevented me from quite seeing the open waters. There are trees round the church with nests of rooks in them. I could look down into these and watch the birds sitting or feeding their young. Some were well advanced and nearly fully feathered. The afternoon was dreadful and I was thoroughly thankful when six o'clock came and I could be relieved as I had become thoroughly tired of the Headquarters and everything else to do with the picquet. There was nothing unpleasant to do: the trouble was that there was nothing to do at all. I do not suppose I shall get this duty again for some time ...

There are plenty of rumours about. We even had one last night that the Germans had landed at Clacton yesterday, I need hardly say it was false or else we should be on the way to meet them. Last Sunday, however, there came a policeman who told us 15 German aeroplanes had left to make a raid on our shores, and that he said was an Admiralty message. Preparations were made and our own aeroplanes were up but the German aeroplanes must have turned back for they never reached England. Of course you can imagine what alarm was made and what talk was caused: people here said they would not go to bed, but they did about 11 o'clock, all except Mr and Mrs Stebbing[3] who stayed up until 1 o'clock. Then Thursday there were strong rumours of another Zeppelin: I went to bed and was not roused until my man came next morning. I have since been told that a Zeppelin came to Harwich but was turned back by our aeroplanes: another man told me this: the people he is billeted with have a private telephone and friends warned them to be ready to turn out. And he said that next morning early he saw three huge Rolls Royce cars, each with a searchlight and an anti-aircraft gun passing. So I think it must be true or else doubt the word of another officer: I myself heard a motor that night humming away which may have been an aeroplane of ours. There is a road at the back of the house with motors passing but the hum I heard was too continuous and deep to be a motor on a road. This morning one of Mr Stebbing's men says he heard guns going off this morning down the Blackwater: perhaps then something has happened. We have been deluged with rumours but few have contained anything that turned out true.

I have had an invitation to the wedding[4] here: it is taking place May 11th: I suppose I must accept though I am afraid I shall feel a stranger. The Miss Stebbing who is to be married is the eldest, named Ethel. She is marrying a Maldon gentleman who has been a rubber planter in Java and returned to take a commission, he is in the 9th Northamptons and is stationed at Penzance. His name is Fitch and his father was Mayor of Maldon. There has been a good deal of shopping here and plenty to talk about and arrange of course and I have heard a good deal about the wedding.

We had a good game of tennis yesterday: it was bright and sunny but there was a cold wind. The girls here are good players: I asked another officer but he did not turn up in spite of his promise. He told me this morning he was engaged in making a bomb proof shelter for the lady at whose house he is billeted and so he could not come. I suppose we are to be here some long time because there are no rumours yet about any changes and generally these are foreknown to some extent anyway. I do not mind if we do stay here but I hope we shall learn a little more about the district than we have done for we have continually been out in the same direction.

I have received shirts and collars and the rest alright: I like the big ties very much. The tennis things are alright and I have found the watch which I am delighted with. It is very good and the figures show up splendidly during the dark. My things have come down from Todd's[5]: they were sent early after I came to Maldon but were returned as insufficiently addressed or something like it. However I have them now and they are all correct. I bought myself a pair of shoes yesterday, price 2/6d: and they look as if they would wear well. I shall be able to get a good deal of tennis while I am here: and the girls have asked me to bring down some of my brother officers. I have promised to do so and they all will be

St Peter's Tower, Maldon where SCB was on picquet duty in April 1915 and saw the nests of rooks in the trees below

delighted to come I know so we ought to be able to make up some parties quite well. Well I must close: I went to church this morning, church parade of course which was over by 10.45. Please give my love to Miss Eden, remember me to Mr and Mrs Guy and Ray and please forward Leslie's address. By the way, please show my letter of last week to Mr and Mrs Guy, if you choose of course, as we have seen so many of Leslie's letters. You can show it to anyone you like as far as I am concerned and do what you like with it. I trust you will not worry about me: I am not a bit afraid and really I felt somewhat disappointed nothing happened the night I was on duty. If another comes I hope to be able to see it if nothing more. Love to Harold, Walter and Aunt and Father: please don't feel anxious because I really do not think there is any reason for it in spite of all rumours: so with especial love to yourself, best wishes to everyone
Your loving son Stanley

Heybridge Hall
[Probably early May 1915]

Dear Mother

Since I last wrote I have had a certain amount of excitement but I hope my wire will have reassured you. I suppose by this time you will have seen some account in the papers: the Times[6] states that so many bombs fell on Heybridge. No one has been hurt and the only damage done round this way has been the breaking of windows and the holes made by the explosion. I will try and tell you what happened to me.

I was woke up by the voices in the house: I heard one of the girls saying it was a Zeppelin dropping bombs on Maldon. I did not get out of bed but lay there half-asleep hoping it was not true as we had been talking and laughing about them at supper and I thought it might be a false alarm. But I soon heard the hum of the motor and I knew it was right and I lay in bed waiting for it to pass. I heard it come closer and heard it dropping bombs and it was an anxious moment wondering where they would fall though I did not somehow think I would be hit. I heard I suppose eight dropped at least, one or two in front of the house and the others behind it. One I heard come down especially loudly and that one exploded with a heavy report and a white flash, I thought in the back garden. One or two more followed but nothing happened as far as I could tell. There was a good deal of light about, flickering but I did not know what it was. I then heard the motor die away and then Mr Stebbing came and called and I got out for all this time I had laid in bed. Everyone was up in their night things, all alarmed: there were fires at the back and the front: we went downstairs and we heard the motor again but it did not come back. Then the bugles went and I put on my trousers, tunic, socks and brought down my boots, put them on and got in to my overcoat and took my hat stick and gloves and went on parade at the alarm post.

There I found some 30 men of my company and there we remained and the battalion gradually formed up, officers and men coming in one or two at a time. It was about 12.30 when I got there. We remained over an hour and then marched off and were dismissed and back in my billet just after two: all were still up and we sat talking for about an hour and I had a biscuit or two and a glass of lemon and went to bed. I did not sleep until about 4 but I had from 4 to 5.30 and 6 to 7.30.

When morning came we realised how near we had come to danger. There was one incendiary bomb 30 yds in front of the house burnt out: this one had been dug out at once and I saw it before going to bed the second time:

there was another at the back of the shed at the bottom of the kitchen garden, no more that 30 yards away: and twenty yards beyond another in a wheatfield, both unexploded incendiary bombs. A little way further on was a burnt bomb. Then less than 100 yds in front of the house was a hole 3 ft deep caused by a big explosive bomb: this was the one that broke the front windows. It fell in soft mud and turned it all up. It did more than 6 men could do in a day's work I should judge. Then less than 300 yds at the back was another great round hole in a corn field: this was more than 8 ft deep, and was shaped like a cone turned upside down.

Besides these, other bombs fell in the river and in a line of 400 yds there must have been a dozen bombs. As far as we can gather only three explosive bombs fell, two of them near us as you see: the other fell in Maldon and shattered a workshop in the Union ... At the lime kiln the lime furnaces were alight and they have openings 12 ft across: these no doubt attracted attention... If one was to draw a line from bomb to bomb, you would find the general direction would make a line right through the house, and undoubtedly the Zeppelin passed right above. When I got out there were three fires at the back and two at the front: these last were at Maldon, near the station close to a timber yard where bright lights were also burning. I think it quite certain the Zeppelin did not know where it was and dropped bombs near any light it could see. The fact that it showered them so close round us who are right at the end of the village with open ground on every side but one shows that and especially if you take into account the great shell wasted on a wheatfield. That was the one of which I saw the flash I suppose.

There was no panic though everyone was alarmed: it is not true people turned out 'as if to see pictures' as some papers put it. Everyone was too scared but as far as I saw no one lost his head. My host was splendid: he was up at once and busy putting out the burning bombs; he rushed out with a sporting gun but the ship was too far away. One of the girls here got up when she heard it and went downstairs and out on the lawn but the two boys were very frightened. I must confess I was alarmed and the time I spent in bed hearing the bombs fall and wondering if they would explode was an unpleasant 2 minutes: but I did not feel a bit excited and kept my head quite well. There was no panic on parade and very little excitement, though all were talking. I was one of the first there but I regret to say I did not take the trouble to put on my braces and felt uncomfortable all the time. I did not feel a bit cold: and I was quite able to manage the men. The Zeppelin came up the Blackwater, passed over Heybridge across to Maldon a mile away and dropped its first bomb there: then it turned round and came back and coming back it gave us our share. The Times says 24 were dropped on Heybridge and Maldon. I fancy there must have been over 30 however; Heybridge had rather more than half. The airship disappeared again down the Blackwater.

Well, I have had a narrow escape and I am proud to say that I had the worst time of all in the battalion, officers and men alike but I think I stood my baptism of fire alright. I must tell my friends in Bristol Battalion how I have scored off them: and if they come again while I am in this house I have made up my mind what to do and I do not think the risk will be great. What struck me most was the extraordinary futility of the affair: the bombs showered round the house and only glass broken. There has been a constant watch kept since and all lights are darkened: but nothing has happened. I am not a bit afraid if they come again but I am sorry to say some here have had a big fright and have not got over it yet. If ever I get to the front I shall give them something extra for the way they frightened the women here.

Well, I expect you have heard enough about it now. I had some pieces to show but the crowds of visitors who came Friday and yesterday have taken all the best bits and I have only second rate relics left. One of the girls here has a fine piece but she has had tremendous trouble to keep it. The usual work has been going on and I am settling down and enjoying myself: we were so many at church parade this morning that along with several other officers I could not find room and had to wait outside for the service.

Please despatch my shirts at once. I am waiting for them. I sent you a card with my address when I sent one to Irene but something must have happened to yours. I have had to write to Todd's again because I have not heard from them but I believe it will be alright now. The boots have come and are a lovely pair, very comfortable indeed. I wore them nearly all day yesterday: and that was only the second time: that shows you how good they are.

Well, to conclude: please remember me to Miss Green and Mr & Mrs Guy and send me Leslie's address. Love to aunt and thank her for her note, the same exactly to Walter, love to Harold and father, and especial love to yourself. I am enjoying myself immensely with four young and pretty ladies for society and decent fellows for officers.

Your Loving Son Stanley.

Heybridge Hall
[Postmarked 10th May 1915]

Dear Mother

Thank you very much for the piece of silver: it will do very nicely and it is now numbered among the wedding presents. They have been coming in well during the last weeks and really make a fine show, most of them being silver. That little brooch however will be unique at any rate: it makes quite a decent little toy: and at least it will be interesting.

The bridegroom is here now: he arrived from Penzance where he has been quartered last night and is sleeping here tonight and last night: the best man arrives tomorrow. He is quite a decent sort, and I like him quite well. He is no taller than myself, I think, though I believe he would be if he held himself straight: he is one of a family of 17 children. His father was Mayor of Maldon and he was born during the Mayoralty, so that he was named Thomas Maldon Fitch[7]. He is a Lieutenant in the 9th Northants who are coming to Colchester which is 15 miles away from here. So I suppose for a bit the people here will see something of him. But his battalion will soon go to the front, I believe.

They have a pony here but until this week they have had no harness: now they have it and the girls manage somehow or other to be going in to Maldon when I go on parade. The result is that I get driven in. The harness came Wednesday I think and every day since I have been driven to parade. It is very enjoyable I can tell you to come on parade fresh and cool, the walk is just far enough to make me sweat by the time I get to the Company parade ground. You are right mother I am very spoilt here: and if Mrs Stebbing had her way it would be worse still, only the girls always remind her that she must not spoil me. On the other hand there is always plenty of chaff and mischief so that there is no likelihood of getting conceited ... Altogether I am having a very enjoyable time. I have heard this week that when the Zeppelin came and I went out without brushing my hair, it was all straight so that one of the girls thought I must curl it in the morning. I did laugh when I was told.

I had tennis on Wednesday and brought down another of our officers: it was a man named Hill this time, a Magdalen man, who has been at Oxford three years. He is quite a good player and as there were some other girls here who are quite good besides my hostesses we had some fine tennis ...

It is hard to realise how far on we are in the year. This year is going the quickest of any in my life. And yet in another sense it seems ages ago to last Christmas. I have done so much in the time. It is very enjoyable here and it is great fun to be an officer: the other officers in my company are very decent especially the Major and the Second in Command, my superiors, and that is the most important point of course. The Second in Command is Lt Grazebrook and he is one of the cleverest men I have ever met. He is married and has had his wife with him here but I am not sure she has not gone back now. He has two little girls I think and was going to take a house here but since the Zeppelin came he has given the idea up as he does not want them frightened. By the way, one little girl of 14 I know here, whose people are friends of the Stebbings asked her mother after the Zeppelin was gone and it was all over whether her hair had turned grey. Her mother, Mrs Gowers, was sharp enough to spot where I came from. She said it was like home to hear me talk and asked if I came from the west country. I said Bristol and then she said she came from Taunton. This is the first time anyone has spoken of my accent or anything of that sort ...

We went on a long march yesterday, 12 miles I expect: fortunately though fine and sunny there was a cool breeze going and so we did not get very hot. All these marches we have to do in full kit, so that I carry my Burberry in straps on my back, and glasses, water bottle and haversack at my sides. The men too carry full pack. On Friday I was hobnobbing with the nobility. Lord Salisbury[8] commands our Division and as we began our work he just drove up and watched us: he asked me several questions and thought I was going wrong but I explained what we were doing. However, the company came in for a wigging, or rather I should say the Captain who was told to alter his arrangements. I heard too another of our captains got one as well. These people, G.O.C.'s and Brigadiers and so on, generally make themselves unpleasant when they do come round. I suppose they do not justify their existence if they don't. Lord Salisbury is a Brigadier General but he commands the Division. Sir John Barnsley[9] commands our Brigade and is a Lt Colonel: and the Brigade Major is Captain Marriott; all are Territorials and not one is a Regular Soldier. Lord Salisbury's appointment has met with a good deal of criticism as he is not a professional soldier. He was I believe a yeomanry officer.

Friday afternoon it was Lord Deerhurst.[10] He is the Brigade Musketry Officer and I had to report to him for duty on the Woodham Mortimer range. He is a Lt Colonel and is very short and fat with small legs. I heard him described as 'a damned old woman' and I quite agree. No one takes any notice of him and it is quite amusing to hear him get angry which he very frequently does. I am afraid he would make me angry if I had a lot to do with him, he is so fussy and so on.

There has been no alarm this week and everything has passed off quietly ...

Well, mother, I hope you will not worry over my money affairs: I shall be all straight soon and I want you to tell me how much the various purchases you have made for me come to and I will send you a cheque. Todd's bill will be no more than £25.6.3., a good deal less than I expected ...


Heybridge Hall
[Probably 16th May 1915]

Dear Mother

I am very sorry to be behindhands with my letter but the hours of church parade have been altered and the place changed so that I do not get anything like the amount of time I used to on Sunday morning. Nothing much has happened besides the wedding during the week but I suppose you will want to hear about that in full. It went off very well and I had a thoroughly good time. It was Tuesday and Tuesday is our long day when we go on to 3 o'clock: but I got leave from my Major to leave parade about 12.00 and got back to the Hall at 1 o'clock: had lunch and changed into cleaner clothes and went to the wedding at 2 o'clock. Unfortunately I was Orderly Officer that day and when the service was over I had to run off to the stores to inspect the rations (this is supposed to be done at 2.30: I got there at 2.45) and I then hurried back and was at the Hall again at 3.15: then onwards I took part in the wedding festivities: it was a lovely day and there was a band on the lawn who had volunteered their services in return for Mr Stebbing's kindness to them at Christmas. Their playing was very good and kept things going: had it not been for them the time would have been very dull: but as it was it was very enjoyable. The bride and bridegroom went off about 5 o'clock and previously, with the help of one of the younger Miss Stebbings I had crept out the back way and had got round behind the car and tied on a pair of white satin slippers. I also was given a jar of vaseline and rubbed it over the leather so that confetti should stick on and when it drove up I put on more still and they went away with a motor bedaubed with large patches of confetti. When they went, the best man and bridesmaids followed them in another motor and more of the bridegroom's sisters in a third: who all gave them a very rousing time at the station so that everybody looked out of the carriage

The wedding of Capt Maldon Fitch and Ethel Stebbing on 11th May 1915.
They are outside Heybridge Hall

windows. In the letters they have written the two declare they think it was I who played with the car: and so when they come back as they will tomorrow they promise me an exciting time. They will be here for a night or so as Mr Fitch's regiment will be at Colchester now. I shall have to be careful for last night I found someone had made a few unnecessary repairs to my pyjamas.

There was a lovely lot of presents: heaps and heaps of silver and everything I should imagine necessary for lunch, dinner, breakfast and tea besides many other handsome gifts. However my little brooch attracted a good deal of attention and I think the bride liked it a lot because she went away wearing it. They spent two days in town and now they are at Torquay. The bridegroom is one of the first draft of his officers to go to the front and I should not be surprised if he does not go at once because there have been large losses in the Northamptons to which he belongs.

There are still alarms here occasionally over Zeppelins but nothing has happened so far... There were strong rumours too that lone Zepps had been brought down but unfortunately that was untrue also. Saturday we had a story there were 11 airships started from Germany and were expected here but nothing happened. I have been told, too, routes have been traced from Heligoland, Hamburg and other air-sheds in Germany to London and that Maldon lies within their danger zone though

Chelmsford does not. I don't know whether it is so: but it seems to me obvious that all the air raids so far have been mere reconnaissance and practice trips meant to test our defences and find the best and clearest route to London ...

Continued Thursday

This is the third instalment of this letter so that you will see we are having a fairly busy time: I cannot somehow find time to write the letter at one sitting; something happens in the evening invariably to break my chance of getting it done, and this is being written before going out to night operations. Nothing much is happening though we have plenty to do. The Major is away for today and the Second in Command of the Company has us: he is much the cleverer of the two and we always have the more interesting time under him. He is the man I was billeted with at Ongar and I got to know in the few days there. I like him and he likes me I think ...

By the way some of Mr Stebbing's men are the queerest of queer characters. There is one old drover who declares he can drive his sheep or cattle better when drunk than when sober. And another often has a day off and turns up on the next and confesses quite calmly he was drunk the day before. This man is called Boss because he has a boss eye: his real name is Taylor but he feels insulted if you don't call him Boss. He sleeps in the stable but is very clean all the same: every morning he washes in a bucket and he always washes his clothes regularly. He was out at once when the Zeppelin came and did a lot of work in putting out blazing bombs and so on. He made quite a lot out of it too: he got pieces of old iron and dipped them in tar and soot and sold them as pieces of bomb. The more I think of it the more wonderful was the escape we had: pieces of bomb have been picked up all round the house but not one of us here was touched. I will finish now: I am really very sorry to be so late with this letter but this has been a busy week ...

What is Walter[11] doing now? It looks as if all will have to take a hand[12] somehow or other and a good job too: I should not like to be out of it. I am very glad I am able to do my part.


Heybridge Hall
[probably 23rd May 1915]

Dear Mother

I am very sorry to have kept you so long without a letter but nowadays I am doing some of the hardest work I have ever done and I do not get very much time to myself and I do not always feel up to the effort of writing a long letter. This afternoon however I have had a sleep and a rest so will try now to give you some news. It was the middle of last week I wrote last I believe.

This week has been almost entirely free of air raid rumours: in fact I believe only once have Zeppelins been reported to our Headquarters and we always get the messages when any have been sighted. But last Friday night we had some excitement. I had been asleep and I was just waking up slowly when a knock came to my door and a voice said 'We can hear a Zeppelin.' I heard people moving and talking on the landing and I got up and slipped on coat and trousers over my pyjamas, picked up my socks and glasses and went downstairs. I had looked at my watch directly I was called and it showed 12.50. When I got down we could hear a Zeppelin sure enough but could see nothing though the noise of the motors was very loud and seemed to fill the sky. We all went to some haystacks near the house which I suppose would be the safest place until the noise disappeared and then we went in and after waiting a little time we all went to bed again at 2 am. The worst of it was that I had to be up again about 5 am but I could not help oversleeping a bit. The Zeppelin we heard had been at Danbury and there the picquet of the 6th Gloucesters had fired at it. I was on the range next day and Lord Deerhurst told us that and he has a house at Danbury. But we have had nothing at all since then. They were very active last week. They visited I believe Hull, Grimsby, Cromer, Harwich, Tilbury and Chatham. At Tilbury I hear they dropped one explosive bomb which fell between two lighters laden with lyddite for the Dardanelles. Near Tilbury is the biggest oil and petrol store in the world and Kynoch's explosives factory so that there is a good deal of anxiety whenever a Zeppelin is seen near that neighbourhood. At Chatham too I hear a large amount of damage was done and two streets were wrecked. The people here in Heybridge Hall are getting used to them and when we all turned out no one was very much alarmed. I was not frightened at all but I was disappointed I could see nothing. I have not seen a Zeppelin yet though I have heard something of them four times now.

We are getting much more work than we used to during the last three weeks: we are now doing our musketry course and that means long hours of duty on the range, from 6.45 to 11am or from 11 to 5pm. Then it requires an hour to get there and an hour to get back. I have had this duty last Saturday, Monday, Wednesday and yesterday. Firing goes on on Sundays too but I do not think we are on tomorrow. I shall be very glad

Soldiers of the Worcestershire Regiment at Maldon in June 1915

Returning from a route march at Epping Camp where SCB was training in September 1915

if we are not. Last Saturday I had from 6.45 to 12.40: I walked back and then with another officer and the two youngest girls here we went over to a farm about six miles away for tennis. We had a splendid time there and returned about 9.45, reached here at 10.15 or so. We had music after it got too dark to play. It was a lovely farm and the people were very nice: they are named Payne and the son is in the 10th Suffolks: he is at Felixstowe and came over during the course of the evening and I liked him. Sunday I was very tired and it was not until evening I felt like doing anything. Then I went to church and as usual when I go to Heybridge church I read the lessons. I noticed the people seemed to be listening: it is a small church and I quite enjoyed doing it: there was no need whatever to strain one's voice to make all hear.

Wednesday I was Orderly Officer. This means being out late because one has to inspect the sentries after 10 o'clock. I was at the range until 5 o'clock: and when I got back I had a lot of running about to do because next day there was an inspection and I wanted to find out the orders. I was not back until after 11 o'clock and then I put my things together. I got up next morning at 10 minutes to five and dressed hurriedly and had breakfast of a sort. The Company fell in at 5.30 and I was a bit late but the battalion formed up at 6.30 and we marched off. We had to go to Boreham 10 miles away and it was a hard job to get the men along as most of them had hardly anything to eat. Fortunately, it had rained the night before so it was cool and not dusty. We marched with three short halts until 10 o'clock. We formed up in Boreham Park[13] and the inspection began at 11. Sir Leslie Rundle, General Officer Commander in Chief of the Central Force under whom we are, was the inspecting officer. He walked round and shook hands with each colonel and asked him to give his men a few exercises. We had to slope arms and I believe we did it fairly well. Then we marched past in double fours, in eights and it was over. It was at least 12.30 before we had ended and we marched along the road until 12.45 when we had 30 minutes halt for lunch. Then we marched back another nine miles and reached home about 4 o'clock. I got back here about 4.30. I stood it pretty well but my feet were very tired that evening. I had a hot bath during the evening and went to bed fairly early. I have seen Jack Langford[14] during the week. I was marching at the head of our company down the hill to the alarm post when I met him billeting his men. I shook hands with him and asked him where he would be and went on but I looked him up during the evening and he came down here with me and we had a chat. He was very envious: he told me they were in hutments at Little Baddow about 7 miles away and to be in a billet like mine was luxury itself compared to the crowded bare little shanties they have to live in. Cox he told me was with their first reinforcement and Lewis who was at St John's was with them too (I saw him on Thursday by the way) and a man named Coates another O B as well ...

I have had to buy some cotton shirts because with this heavy tunic, wool is an impossibility in this warm weather. If we were to be sent to the Dardanelles we should have to buy drill tunics and breeches for the heat ...

I am enclosing a piece of bomb in box. It was found out on the meadows some little time after the raid so that it had time to grow rusty. It was found about 200 or 250 yds from either bomb hole and some little distance from the house, so that you can see what we had round our heads on that night. It really is a wonder no one was hurt or no damage worth speaking of was done. I hope aunt will like her little present. I am very sorry to be so late with it but I hope she will find it useful ...


Heybridge Hall
1st June 1915

Dear Mother

As you will see from the address which may rather surprise you I am still in Maldon and shall be until further notice: and I do not know when that will come. It slipped my mind that I had informed you I was leaving here or you should have heard from me before now. However it happened thus: last Thursday night I saw in orders a notice that a machine gun course was to assemble at Bisley on May 31st and that I was to attend. So Friday night I was busy, wrote to the bank for money and went and found out what I was to do and wrote to you. But next morning I was informed a note had come down from Brigade Headquarters that I was not to attend. So I did not go ...

It is a very interesting but quite a hard course I believe. Machine guns are enormously important in battle nowadays and I have heard, though I do not know if it is true, we are to have 8 per battalion, two to a company, instead of 1 as in the old time. When a machine gun is found, infantry steer clear of it all round and artillery is turned on until the machine gun is out of action. It is said though whether true I cannot say, that the average life of a machine gun officer in battle is 20 minutes. Everybody's attention is turned on the guns and so the gun crews do not stand much chance. The man who had the best report after his course is the one who will be appointed machine gun officer here.

Every day this week and last except Saturday we officers do bayonet drill, prodding at sacks with bayonets and jumping over trenches and stabbing sacks on the other side and so on. We have a very good instructor and the work is interesting though it seems to lengthen the days' work enormously. We shall finish this week it is expected at any rate. All subalterns have to attend and the captains can if they like.

Last week a change was made in the organisation of the battalion. The Home Service men[15] were fallen out and formed into a separate company under their own officers. They make just about half a company and it is a curious thing they have quite a large number of N.C.O.'s especially sergeants among them. These of course are elderly men who are not quite up to foreign service. But it has meant that I have lost both my Company Officers. Both Major Watson and Mr Grazebrook are Home Service and I am sorry to be parted from them; however I have Captain Boucher and Lieutenant Gough as my superiors now. They are both very nice but they will run things with more precision than there used to be: they will be rather stricter too. However I do not mind that and I think I shall learn a lot from both of them as they are both good and clever men. They are of course Foreign Service Volunteers ...

We have alarms here about Zeppelins still and though we have had none over Maldon since I wrote we have had them very close twice since I wrote last. Wednesday last week, the Zeppelins came to Southend as perhaps you remember. Well, we had all gone to bed and I was asleep but just awaking when a knock came on my door and one of the girls here said they could see flashes and hear explosions. So I said alright I would get up and come down. I slipped on a coat and did so and found all the family out in the garden looking towards Southend, down the Blackwater. Shoeburyness and Southend are quite close and farther down still is Thameshaven where are the largest petrol stores in the world and Kynoch's explosives factory. Shoeburyness is the station where naval guns are tested so that there are plenty of guns all along and we often hear them. Well when I came down (it was about 11.10) we could hear all the guns going off all the way around and as we watched, we saw lights appear in the sky and go out, just a flash which showed for quite a perceptible moment. These I think must have been shells bursting. I also saw sharp flashes off the ground which I am sure from what I saw here were bombs exploding. The firing went on until about 11.35 and then ceased: it was not continuous but in bursts and came from many points. The Zeppelins hovered motionless in one place over Southend for quarter of an hour; the firing commenced punctually at 11 o'clock with very rapid reports and then continued as I have described ...

I have received a cheque today for 2 guineas, subsistence allowance for April at the rate of 1/9d per day: I have heard from Cox & Co and they have £74 for me: £50 allowance for kit and £24 for pay up to May 31st. I have instructed them to remit all monies due to me to my bank in Oxford and I have written to Oxford to tell them to expect them. I expect to hear shortly they have done so: you see that this is alright also.

We are not likely to move from Maldon for another five weeks I believe: but the Home Service men may move at any time: when we go we shall go to Salisbury Plain or somewhere else for brigade and divisional training: and I suppose we are not likely to go abroad until October at least. Maldon Fitch will go to the front any day now: he is on the next draft and may go to the Dardanelles or to Flanders, he doesn't know which. He and his wife are in Colchester at present: when he goes she will return home most likely.

Please mother do not worry about me: I am having a very good time in Maldon and of course all these alarms are part of a soldier's life, and will be very good training, and it is only what we are meant for. If I am to come out safe I shall not be hurt here; if not, it is one of the risks I must take and it is only what I knew I should have to face. I shall be glad to hear what you are all doing, and I hope you will all do something to help the country along because the help of everyone, men and women alike will be wanted. I hope both Harold[16] and Walter will take some share in it all, some way or other: I feel very angry when I see all the young men I do see round here out of uniform. Those who wait till they are forced to join will have a much worse time and will be treated with far less consideration than those who volunteered. So it will be best I think to offer one's services in some form soon because I fully believe conscription[17] or compulsory service in some form will be here before long.

I am afraid this letter will be too late to go out tonight: but I hope you will forgive me and not be anxious. Please think of all the mothers who have sons in the battle line and be thankful you have your family safe so far... The letter I received was from Mr Powell[18] at Oxford and I am going to reply to it as soon as I can. He tells me of the St John's dons and men I knew; they seem all to be in training now though I see two men I know have won prizes in Oxford this term. It is better to be serving than to win all the prizes in Oxford now I think ...

Heybridge Hall
[Probably mid-July 1915]

Dear Mother

Just a line now to let you know I was inoculated[19] Tuesday evening and am quite alright. As I told you I have had 48 hours leave and go on parade tomorrow morning again. The operation was not painful and has hardly affected me at all: I did not sleep very well after it but I am not sure that was not due to the hot night: I got up about 8.15 and felt alright. I felt a little lazy and my arm was a bit stiff and my shoulder: I was inoculated in the shoulder. Last night I slept excellently and today am quite alright and the stiffness has entirely disappeared by now. So you see I am not at all hurt. I have to be done with a stronger dose within 10 days or a fortnight: but of course I shall be more prepared to meet that and I do not anticipate anything worse than I have had this time. However we shall see ...


Heybridge Hall
[Postmarked 20th July 1915]

Dear Mother

I am very glad to tell you I am not in any way affected by inoculation: I am feeling quite fit and well and am in quite good spirits so that you can see there is nothing the matter with me. I suppose that at the end of this coming week or the first day in next I shall be a second time dosed with typhus bacteria: the first dose I am told is 2,000,000 germs and the second 3,000,000: the second is the worse but then of course one is fortified against that at the first time. I do not feel a bit alarmed and after it I am entitled to leave. So much for that then.

This past week we have finished our musketry course and are now free for other work. Monday was Field Firing and I had to take charge of our company contingent. Field Firing is the most realistic of all the practices we carry out. We fire at targets concealed on a piece of ground and we have to advance towards them just as we would if they were firing against us. We use ball ammunition of course and so we have to be very careful. It is a wonder to me no one was hurt as the men did not think a bit ...

The battalion is much below full strength as we have sent away men to France and officers too: they went away the Sunday after I returned early in the morning, six of them. Then all the Home Service Officers and men and the men unfit for Foreign Service have been sent to Clacton where with similar contingents from the 8th Worcesters and 4th & 6th Gloucesters they form the 83rd Provisional Battalion. Col Wheeler is to take command as I suppose he is too old for foreign service. We said goodbye to him last Friday and he left Maldon on Saturday. I was very sorry as he was a nice old man and to him I owe my commission. Lt Col Danks has command now: I should think he was considerably younger: and I think he will make a good C.O. as I think he will keep a firmer hold on things than Col Wheeler. Altogether the battalion is thoroughly disorganised[20] more officers and men being wanted: and it will take a little time to get going again …

This week we are digging trenches and shall have some trench warfare. We are digging against the 8th Worcesters and then when the trenches are ready we shall both get into them and see what we can do against the others: if they are ready in time we are to have dummy bombs to throw. These are made of paper or something and flare up on touching earth so that we shall at least be able to see how we get along with that. The trenches are 80$yds$ apart and these last two days we have been digging hard: we are making a firing trench with a communicating trench behind, then a support trench 25$yds$ behind that. If this was in Flanders there would be reserve trenches and other trenches again behind that but time of course prevents any very elaborate scheme: which is not at all necessary for our purposes. I think the men quite like it as a change and I find it quite interesting myself too to superintend their work: fortunately one of the last lectures I had in Oxford was on entrenching and I feel I know quite enough to be able to watch and care for the workings properly …

Sunday afternoon we went for a bathe, the two younger girls and myself and we met another party of people we know: two other officers of our battalion and the people they are with, all very jolly. We had a very merry time: we bathed and then six of us went for a row. We did not get back until nearly six. Then we had to have tea and it was too late for me to go to church. Of course I was on church parade in the morning. I was sorry to miss the evening service …

Tonight we are on night work: we are having a march and shall be back soon after 10 o'clock. Tomorrow we are having a long day digging, 9.30-2.30 and then we finish for the day …

We have had one alarm here as a test: it occurred while I was away but soon we are to have another. We have all to dress and go out ready equipped for marching off: it is a test of course to see how long we shall take to assemble. The next will occur shortly but when we do not know exactly. Later on we are to be mobilised. What that is I do not know as we only heard about it this morning. The whole Central Force is to undergo the test however. I have heard that the Government expect a raid or an attempt at landing on these shores. This may be something to do with it: or again, it may be only a trial as they have at Aldershot. The rumour is that we are to go to India. I hope not or that if we do I shall be sent to France beforehand with a draft. I should not like to be idling in India at a time like this ...

I think I have run out of news now: there is nothing more to tell that I can think of. Thank you very much for the letter. I am quite well in every way and enjoying myself too ...

P.S. I have had to spend nearly £6 on one or two things: a proper regulation kitbag, a sleeping valise and mattress for my camp bed this week. Now I think I am all set up ready for camp at any moment.


Heybridge Hall
[Postmarked 1st August 1915]

Dear Mother

I have been very busy indeed since I last wrote to you and shall be too during the coming week. We are not however going into camp tomorrow as the ground is not ready and the Colonel of Engineers who has to prepare it says he cannot get it ready for some days. But we may be in before the week is out though I think it doubtful: however we shall go I suppose as soon as possible but for the time being all is uncertain. So I remain here until we know definitely.

Captain Boucher has gone for a week's leave and Butcher who is a Lieutenant and next in command is Assistant Adjutant: he too is going on leave for a week tomorrow. The next senior is myself: so for a week I am in charge of the Company and I shall have to look after it for that time. Already I have had to take on a big job which is not quite finished. The Company Commander is responsible that every man in his company is correct in every way. In fact the only thing he is not responsible for is the man's spiritual welfare: for all else he has to answer. He has to be father, mother and every relation to his men. He is their lawyer and banker, doctor to some extent and clothier: he is responsible for their food and welfare in every respect and if they are in any trouble whatsoever he has to see to it. That is what I have to do this week. Yesterday for instance a man came to me and wanted to go home as his wife had just been confined and he wanted to see her. I had to read the letter and a very pathetic letter it was too. So I got him special leave for it and got him a railway voucher, return journey at single fare, and then he said he had no money to pay even the single fare. I had then to take him to the Company Quartermaster Sergeant and he gave him 15/- to get him home: and the money will be made up by weekly stoppages from his pay. So he went and was all provided for.

Yesterday too a message came from Divisional Headquarters that we were to send a draft of 140 men or so if we could. Our strength is 785 and we had to find these men and still leave 600 fit for service overseas. So we had to order a medical inspection and all this came when the men had been dismissed for the day. We got some together and sent some off last night for inspection: the rest we had to parade for it today instead of church parade. This business meant for me an afternoon's work in the Company office, and a parade at 5 o'clock when the men were examined: I was present and got off at 6.30 pm. Tonight now that is over I have to pick 25 men to put on this draft and so I shall have more work. I am going to the office at 8.30 pm to see to it. The draft will have to be ready to go to the Continent at short notice, and they are getting for them the requisite equipment and special boots. Nothing has yet been said about officers. I do not expect they want any as we have sent 8 out just lately but they may... However, we shall hear I suppose: more may have to go and perhaps I shall be one if I pass the tests. Looking round the battalion, there are not many subalterns senior to me and some of these they will keep back so that my chances of going soon are large... I am not sorry to think I may have a chance of going out and doing my share soon. I think at any rate I am at least as efficient as the officers sent out and I don't think I should be hopelessly lost if I have to go soon ...

I was able to get a bathe this afternoon in the river before the house as the tide came in. A whole party bathed; we changed in our rooms, put on a coat and walked across the lawn and tennis court and then into the river just the other side and came back and changed and dried in our rooms again. Tomorrow we have a half day though I do not feel very optimistic that I will be able to have all that time off. I shall think of you and your Bank Holiday and remember the day we had last year. Last night passed quietly though I believe there have been some raids lately: and one of our officers declares he heard a Zeppelin close here last week. He heard it twice and so certain was he that he got out and put a respirator on his dressing table; and he is not a man who is at all jumpy or alarmed at trifles and if he thought he heard one he's likely to be right.

There is talk we are to have a new C.O. He is to be a man named Poynter and the only Poynter to be found in the Army list is a Captain of the Special Reserve of Scots Guards. If that is so, he will make us all jump about pretty shortly and pull things here a bit tighter and we certainly require it.

Thank Harold for his letter: I trust they had a good holiday and tell Walter if he can to write me a line from camp. I believe Walter could if he would get into the Army now as they have issued orders men are not to be rejected for such things as eyesight.[21] I do not know if he will but if he does, he will be welcome as all men will be wanted. I daresay he could get a commission if he went about it the right way, Dr Norwood and Mr Gardiner ought to be able to help him in that and he deserves it as much as many a man I saw in Oxford. But I would sooner lose anybody than Walter in this war, though what we are fighting for is so sacred that any sacrifice ought to be made. I hope Harold will join a training corps: it will all help and if he can do war work as well this winter, he will be doing his part.

Well, mother, you must not be discouraged: you ought to be glad you are able to give your sons and if German mothers can lose their sons simply to make Germany dominant in Europe, we ought to be able to do more to end all the old barbarous ideas Germany stands for and to make it plain the strong shall no longer override the weak. Well, mother, my dearest love to father and yourself and please do not be anxious about me: I shall be alright and if I do go soon, as I hope, you ought to be proud to say you have a son at the front. Well, goodbye for tonight with my dearest love to all at home …


Heybridge Hall
[Postmarked 8th August 1915]

Dear Mother
I have had a very busy week this week but now Captain Boucher is back once more and I shall be relieved of a lot I have had to do. He returned last night and I saw him and gave an account of the week's doings and I think he was satisfied: at any rate he seemed pleased. Even if I had not had all that work to do we should have had a full time because we had two big ceremonial parades, one on the anniversary of the Declaration of War, last Wednesday, and the other on Friday when we went to Chelmsford to be reviewed by Lord Kitchener[22] and of course I had to get the Company ready for both occasions. On Monday, we went digging at the trenches: Tuesday was wet so we did not have much to do: Wednesday we were

inspected, Thursday digging and Friday we went to Chelmsford. Yesterday we had a short parade and today the usual Sunday service ...

Friday was of course a much bigger thing: we had to march 13 miles or so and be on the ground by 9.45. So we paraded at 3.30 am: the Company fell in at 3.10 and the battalion formed up at 3.30 and we marched off. We marched until 7.45 or so: then we halted on a place called Galleywood Common and had breakfast: tea was made there but no other cooking was allowed as we had no time. Practically every man in the battalion had to go: and although the parade was so early and the men had so little sleep only two fell out on the way there: and we arrived in good order. The packs were put on a wagon so the men had much less to carry than they would have done in the ordinary course of active service and of course too we took no ammunition. After breakfast we had to make the companies equal in strength and size them, that is we put the tallest men on the flanks and the shortest in the centre. We then marched off to the review ground, which was in Hylands Park, Sir Daniel Gooch's[23] place. There the whole division formed up: the Engineers and Artillery in front and then behind them the Infantry and behind them the transport wagons, horses and mules. We got there just before ten o'clock: the officers took post in front of the battalion and then we waited: Lord Kitchener arrived at 10.50 and we saluted: we had to wait for another 20 minutes and he came on parade. I suppose meanwhile he had been looking into the divisional records or something. There were staff officers everywhere and Sir Leslie Rundle watched the Division form up.

When Lord Kitchener came, he rode along the front of the line of artillery and engineers starting from the right: he then came round the left by a drive and was greeted by applause from the spectators. We were on the left of the line of infantry, the 8th Worcesters on the extreme left then ourselves, then the Gloucesters and then the other brigades. Our Brigadier let himself be caught napping and had the brigade still standing at ease: and the C.O. of the 8th Worcesters was worse: his battalion was standing at ease when Lord Kitchener rode right up to them. As we were next we had just time to get right: the officers meanwhile had returned to their companies and as 'A' Company was in front I had a splendid view. Lord Kitchener came along the front and then between our two battalions and then back again and so passed along the front. He rode next along the rear of the brigade and then off to the saluting point. The Artillery and Engineers went first and we had to wait for them to pass: then we marched off. We marched past in eights, that is two columns of fours together up a broad drive in the park. As we went by Lord Kitchener had

Col Danks called up to him and chatted to him as we went by. Then we marched off and out of the park to Galleywood Common again where we had dinner.

Lord Kitchener had a large staff with him, between 20 or 30 altogether I should think: chief among them being Sir Leslie Rundle. He was riding a splendid horse, pure white: he was in khaki with heaps of gold lace on his cap and collar and of course he had the red band of the Staff: he wore a triple row of ribbons among which I especially noticed the Egyptian medals. He was much stouter than when I saw him five years ago. In fact he could only be called fat, and I must confess he looked a brute. He looked as if he had a very bad temper: his face was red like all these high officers and puffy and he had a large double chin. But he looked very determined and masterful and he was evidently a man who had his own way in his own affairs and he seemed as if he would look after everybody else too. He was a fine looking man but spoilt by looking bad-tempered. Perhaps you have seen pictures of the review in the papers as some were given: and also accounts were allowed for the first time I think ...

Yesterday, Saturday morning I saw a man I used to know at school named Hall in a motor in Maldon High Street: he is a 2nd Lt in the 4th Gloucesters and Brigade Orderly Officer and in constant attendance on the Brigadier. I asked him if anyone knew what Lord Kitchener thought of it: he said no one knew that as Lord Kitchener said nothing but Sir Leslie Rundle he said was immensely delighted. As we were talking the Brigadier came out of a shop and jumped into the car. I saluted and he asked me if I was alright. I said yes and then he inquired if the men were tired and if we were having a rest and I said yes to both questions ...

P.S. I received the Chronicle[24] this morning and am very pleased: I have been reading it during the day.

# FROM BISLEY TO BRENTWOOD

Between the beginning of September 1915 and the end of February 1916 Stanley was posted to places near London: to Bisley where he did a course in machine gun work; to Epping where he spent a month in camp; then back to Bisley again for another short course and finally to Brentwood for four months where he was billeted with the hospitable Robinson family and his men lived in the local school buildings.

The keynote for the whole of this period is frustration. There is not a single reference in letters home to the sacred cause they are fighting for, to the need for sacrifice or to pride in serving the country. Perhaps Stanley's mother does not need any reassurance because he is not in any danger and the prospect of service at the front is remote. There are rumours they might be sent to India or Persia or even France but nothing definite. All the time they are losing men to munitions work and not until late January 1916 do 324 recruits arrive to join the battalion to bring it up to strength, all needing to be trained and made fit for fighting; so any departure is delayed by several months. Senior officers leave for the front and are replaced by men who do not stay long. The most disturbing aspect of all the confusion is the comment in late January that they are hoping to obtain more equipment but there are only rumours of the arrival of rifles, machine guns and rangetakers; there is no sign of the real thing.

In this situation it must have been difficult to keep morale high; there were endless practices in musketry, trench digging and bayonet fighting; parades, marches and night exercises. But what was the plan? Where was it leading? As Stanley wrote in January 1916: '... it is tiring to be in England training, training all the time; it is about time we were off.'

Bisley Camp
Brookwood
Surrey
[Postmarked 29th August 1915]

Dear Mother

I am sorry not to have written you any real news for so long but I have been very busy all this week. I arrived here on Monday last all safe and sound and have been getting on quite well ever since. Already I have had one exam and got through it quite well ...

I was not originally detailed to come here: another officer was to be sent but he was then transferred to another course and on Thursday night it was notified in orders I was to attend. So I had to get ready quickly. When I arrived I found Langford here: he was just starting on the last week of a machine gun course which is now ended and he has left. There are two sergeants of our battalion here, and an officer of the 8th Worcesters and two sergeants with him.

We are lodged in hutments: these hutments are run in blocks together, divided up into so many little rooms and we have one each. I have a little room larger than the pantry at home but nothing like as large as the scullery: and here I have my bed and a desk and chest of drawers and wash stand. It is the smallest space possible to live in: here I have to do all my work in the evenings. We are quite close to the butts and firing is going on every day and we do not notice it now. There are club houses round belonging to the various Rifle Clubs and we use them in different ways. The Middlesex and North London Rifle Association club house is the mess-room for the officers musketry class and it contains a bar and writing room as well and has a verandah in front. It is a very pleasant building and fairly large. Here we have breakfast at 8 o'clock, lunch at 1, tea at 4 o'clock and dinner at 7 o'clock. Other club buildings are used as classrooms and the offices of the National Rifle Association are the Headquarters of the Musketry course. I have a servant, an employee of the National Rifle Association who looks after my clothes and hut along with those of other men in neighbouring huts. We are divided into squads of 10 men each under an instructor. I am in No 1 squad as we are taken alphabetically and have as instructor Company Sgt Major Humphrey. Major Richardson is in command of the whole show: he is a noted shot and musketry expert. We have as our classroom the club house of the Surrey Rifle Association and do a lot of work on the verandah.

We have to work here: Oxford was nothing like it. We have instruction from 9-1 in the morning with a break of 20 minutes or slightly more in the middle: and again from 2 to 4. Then we have to prepare for next day in the evening and enter the notes we have taken during the day into a permanent note book. By the time four o'clock comes I am generally feeling tired and so I rest until 5.30 or so: then I work to 7 o'clock and then start again after dinner at 8.30 and work up to 10 or 10.30. I get to bed just after eleven and get up between 7 and 7.30. This means 9 hours work a day at least and more sometimes. At Oxford I used to try and do six or seven if I had anything special to think about. However, it is not quite all sitting down and thinking.

We start at 9 o'clock with one or two musketry exercises and later we sometimes go out and do a little outdoor work. But the majority of the work is lectures and instruction, both of which require the taking of notes and these have to be transferred to a book during the evening. We have already had one exam but 4 more are to come which will all be harder. I got through quite well. It was on the mechanism and care of the rifle: and to know the mechanism required a very clear head and it was quite hard to master. Fortunately I knew something of it before I came down here ...

The country round here is very pretty: yesterday afternoon I went for a short walk along the Basingstoke Canal which is really extremely pretty, woods coming down right to the water's edge. The soil is very sandy: in fact it is sand and there is a lot of heather and gorse about and plenty of trees and bushes. We are about six miles from Aldershot and there are numbers of troop everywhere ...

There have been several names I know in the casualty lists lately. One is an Old Bristolian, G C Machon, cousin of Roy Machon who was wounded at the Dardanelles. He is a lieutenant in the 5th Welsh Regt. Another name you will know is Philpotts, Lieutenant 7th Gloucesters, Tony Summers' friend: he too has been wounded at the Dardanelles. The 7th Gloucesters are a battalion of Kitchener's army: the 5th Welsh a Territorial Unit. Another man in the 7th Gloucesters who has died of wounds came from St Johns: his name is G R Johnson and his father was at one time a master at the Bristol Grammar School and he himself knew Mr Ford and one or two others. Another St Johns man, R M Humphries has been wounded belonging to a Welsh Territorial Battalion: and another St Johns man has been killed in France. To see his name gave me rather a shock as he was so well known in the college and the varsity. He was the college rugger captain in my first year and he nearly won his blue at footer and tennis. He was a Merchant Taylor's Scholar and a great character in the college being famed for his all-round 'heartiness'. His name was Roe and he belonged to the 7th Rifle Brigade. It was a shock to me I suppose because I could remember him so well, he was one of the men you could remember well. He was clever too and had just won a place in the civil service and a position was being kept for him. He was one of the best men in every way in the College ...

The 7th Worcesters with the rest of the brigade will I suppose go in to camp at Epping this week: and when I rejoin I shall have to go to Epping. I presume I have said good-bye to Maldon and Heybridge Hall now for good: because no one expects to go back to Maldon when we return from Epping. The battalion is to be in Epping a month. When that is finished all the Division will have been in camp for a period and we shall be ready for something more but what it will be no one knows. My Captain says we are quite as well trained as the first 7th when they went out, so perhaps we shall be moving before long. No one knows but India is mentioned and some of the Territorials already there are being moved away. But it may easily be somewhere else and I have seen that the 5th Somerset LI is in the Persian Gulf now ...

P.S. I am enclosing key of trunk which I hope has now reached home.


Bisley Camp
[Postmarked 5th September 1915]

Dear Mother

This week we have been continuing the work of last week and developing it: there is nothing very much to say about it except that we went on to the range and fired on Friday. I did not do very well as my rifle was not firing according to its sighting but I felt very pleased with myself because I found out how to sight it to be accurate although it was generally too late to be of much use. The experience and knowledge were very valuable and I fired quite steadily. Nearly all my shots were on the centre line as they should be: and if I could have found out more quickly how to sight my rifle I should have made a good score.

Tomorrow we have three exams: one a practical exam in instructing a squad: we have each to instruct and show a squad how to do certain things while an examiner watches, and notes good or bad points. We have ten minutes each of it. The next exam is in judging distance and we shall have to judge four distances I expect. The third exam is in the use of a range finding instrument called the Barr and Stroud Infantry Range-Finder. I don't think I have told you about it. It is 31 inches long and you set it on a small tripod, it has two lenses at each end and you look through two glasses in the middle of an instrument. You see there two pictures of the object you are looking at, one upside down and the other normal: then you select on the picture the object of which you want to know the distance and work a screw until the pictures of it in the top and bottom view meet and as you move, disappear into each other without any overlapping. Then you look at a scale and you round off the distance. This instrument is the one used in the army at present: there are four to a battalion, one to each company. They cost £38 each and are very easily damaged: and if they are damaged they must be sent back to the maker for repairs. This infantry one will take ranges up to 20,000 yds with greater or less exactness as the distance is small or large ...

Another thing we see a lot of here is flying and aeroplanes. The flying school at Farnborough is no more than 5 miles away and aeroplanes are constantly passing over this way. Sometimes we see half a dozen a day: and one day this week I saw 4 on the horizon all in one spot up at the same time. They are generally travelling very fast and I should say though I do not know that the Army aeroplanes nowadays are much speedier than they were two or three years ago. They are all bi-planes as monoplanes are nothing like steady enough for Army work ...

I see from the papers that Philpotts whom I told you of last week has died of his wounds but perhaps you have heard from the Vicar. I don't think I have seen any other names this week that I know but I see the Gloucester Hussars have been in action and I shall keep a watch to see that Harding, Stallon and Langford are all safe ...

Three or four of us had a very interesting talk with Major Richardson who is Chief instructor here one day this week. He was talking to us about munitions. He said people did not realise the enormous advantage the Germans had over us there. In the days before the war they used to supply not only their own army but Italy and the Balkans, the South American and other States while we only supplied ourselves. Then too they hold the Belgian ammunition factories at Liege and one of the French factories at Chalons: and it would be years before we could match them. Japan could send munitions but not very much and they stopped doing so soon after the war broke out as they feared a war with China; but they had just started to provide Russia with ammunition and other requirements. The United States could supply a large amount as they had always sent stuff to the South American states and so we were able to draw a lot from them but we had to pay fancy prices for it all. He said too that now we were getting to work and the work was exceedingly well organised but it would take us years to be equal with Germany. France had realised the problem and had been preparing for some months now. Major Richardson is a splendid shot: he always makes one of the English team which shoots at the Olympic Games or elsewhere ...


Wintry Park Farm Camp
Epping
Essex
[Postmarked 19th September 1915]

Dear Mother
There is not very much news to give you: we have had no further excitement this week. The bombs were all dug out of their holes by the Gloucesters and taken up: they were found to be between 7 and 8 ft deep in the earth. They were very heavy, more than 140 lbs each and the Engineers reckoned from the holes they made they must have struck the ground with a force of more than 72 tons. They were excavated and brought up and I saw one of them, they were nearly round in shape and about 1 ft thick: with a brass fuse on top. The Gloucesters tried to explode it but it did not come off. I watched. They took the bomb to a field at the top of a hill a mile from the camp and placed it in a hole 7 or 8 ft deep, took off the fuse and fastened a slab of gun cotton on it with a wire 20 ft long or so. Then round the bomb in the hole they placed sand-bags and built up a wall about 3 ft all round and last of all piled brushwood on the top. Then we were all told to stand clear and so we all got into an old trench about 100 yds away: then the Engineers lighted the wire and bolted. The wire burned at the rate of 2 inches in 6 seconds I think: however there was enough wire to last four minutes. So we waited: then we heard a report and a small cloud of white smoke floated up. It was the gun cotton exploded: everyone made a rush for the hole and the sand-bags were soon torn up and it was found the bomb was unhurt except for a large rent in it. We found it filled with a yellow powder: the Engineer Captain who was in charge did not know what the stuff was: he lit some and it burned quietly. I then came away as it was getting near time for the officers' mess but we heard more attempts to explode the bomb. Last of all the Engineer officer was seen driving off with the bomb lying on the back seat of his motor. I brought back a little of the stuff to the mess: but no one knew what it was though everyone had a look. I have since heard the bombs were meant to be asphyxiating: but somehow or other they failed to do anything at all ...

Here in this camp are plenty of Old Boys. There is Hannam, Capt in the 4th Gloucesters, Hall Lt of the same but now the Aide-de-Camp of the Brigadier and Staff Captain-to-be. In the 6th there are the two Langfords, the elder is Captain in Command of B Company, the younger, the one who was at school with us, is now appointed machine gun officer. Lewis is there, the very tall man you may remember and Cox who is Lt there and Coates, besides Lt Col Carter himself. Ridler is in the 4th Gloucesters so that we make a fairly large crowd. There is a rumour going round that our battalions are to stay in England and take in a number of conscripts to make us up to strength and train them. Conscription is to come in in October[1] according to this rumour. I think it is nothing even though the Brigadier has spoken of it because it is not even known yet whether the Cabinet has taken any decision on the matter yet. But at any rate I think it true we shall remain here all the winter as we are as a Division very much below strength and we have still a lot of training to do. Our new C.O. is changing our methods a good deal: he is an old Cavalry officer of the Indian Army but he left that some years ago: he then went on the staff on the Infantry side for a time but had retired when war broke out. He was for some time recruiting officer in Dorset and then he came to us. He wants everything to be done at once; and the thing he hates most is slowness ...

Wintry Farm Camp
[Postmarked 3rd October 1915]

Dear Mother

Thank you very much for your letter. I was very glad to hear what you all are doing and I suppose now we shall all be settling down for the winter and I can see you are already beginning to at home. We shall not be quite settled until we leave here and are put into billets. We are not to leave here yet as far as we know at present. Monday October 18th is the date mentioned now and then we are to go to Brentwood according to our present arrangements. We shall be billeted there and spend the winter there I suppose. We shall be busy at Musketry, Bomb throwing, Machine gun work, Trench digging and Bayonet fighting I suppose, for the Colonel said those he considered the essential work for us. And when we get there he is going to start a riding school for subalterns so that before Christmas I hope to be able to ride. It will be very useful to learn that as there are all sorts of jobs in the Army which require a man who can ride and so perhaps I shall get a chance for something good, who knows? But we are to stay here for another fortnight as Brentwood is not ready for us yet. The Brigadier and his Staff Captain went over to see whether we could go there last Friday and found it was not prepared or else we should have gone this Tuesday or Wednesday. We have had very cold and bitter weather for more than a week now but today is quite bright and warm: if however it turns cold again it may result in our leaving here quickly as the Brigadier likes to be comfortable: in the cold weather he was heard to observe, 'The sooner we get out of this hole the better' and the morning after the gale we had this week the Brigade Staff was very peevish as the Brigade-Major was lame from a fall from his horse. The Staff Captain had been unable to sleep from cold and the Brigadier could get no breakfast as no fires could be lit in the winds ...

Wednesday morning, the day after our wet night, we could do nothing. It was Sports Day but they were postponed at once and they are to come off this Thursday next. Later on during the morning the bugle was blown from Brigade Headquarters for the Brigade to fall in: and when we were formed up the Brigadier came on parade with the Brigade Major and a party from the 3rd Army Headquarters ... The Colonel stepped forward and introduced Sir George Marks,[2] M P for a Cornish constituency. Sir George then got up and made a short speech on the munitions question[3] and told the men they could serve in a double capacity as soldiers and mechanics in the workshops and receive the usual allowances civilians receive when living away from home. He then asked men who wished to take up this work and thought they were qualified to send in their names to the Orderly Room. The A.D.C. told me they had been down to Southampton the day before to try to settle a strike going on in a shipbuilding yard where two destroyers and seven submarines were being built: the men were out and the ships idle and they had gone down to try what they could do. Sir George Marks I hear is a large engineer: he is a Liberal and has just come back from the front ...

Friday was another cold morning with a frost: but it turned out beautifully sunny and bright: we went out for a route march southwards and went through some of the prettiest countryside I have seen in England. The country all the way round here is very pretty indeed. It is all agricultural land, all under the plough or for pasturage except that it is dotted with woods: woods are everywhere and some of them are quite large: they break up the landscape and vary it considerably. The country is not at all flat either. It is all small hills and slopes and there are several points over 300 ft high. It is no wonder I think that the Londoner spends his Saturday or Sunday in Epping Forest: it must be a blessing to have such fine country at London's door. Londoners pass through here in crowds on Saturday and even more so on Sunday: on Sundays the road outside the camp is a long procession of various motors and horse vehicles ...

Friday evening I went to see the pictures in Epping after mess: but the entertainment was poor and there was nothing very much in the pictures except one of a trial flight by a French dirigible[4]: and it was interesting to see that the French have dirigibles besides the Germans. It was worthwhile to pay 1/- to go to a place where it was possible to be really warm for a night and as far as that went I really enjoyed myself. As to my coming home I think there is no chance of that for three weeks but when we leave here I am going to try for it. I spoke to the Adjutant about it yesterday and he said the Colonel was sure to grant it if I was in time in making my application. So I hope to be down before very long and you can be sure I am looking forward to it thoroughly: and I mean this time not to disappoint you ...


Wintry Farm Camp
[Probably mid-October 1915]

Dear Mother
...Tomorrow is to be the Brigade Sports and the Brigadier has promised a cup to the battalion which gets the most points. We already have got some and trust to get more, and fancy ourselves pretty well. One event has already been run and we have got most of the points, 9 out of 15. This was a 7 miles marathon race and two of our runners came in for the two leading places: one was a Lance-Corporal and the other a Company Quartermaster Sergeant. The 6th Gloucesters and the 4th Gloucesters got 3 points each. We ran off our heats on Sunday and some very good form was shown so that we are hopeful: and one of our officers is I should think a 'dead cert' for the half mile.

The 4th Gloucesters lodged a complaint against our two runners in the marathon as they said they had been paced: and of course the matter had to come up before the Sports Committee. This was done on Sunday evening at 6 o'clock and took place in the Mess of the 4th Gloucesters. I had to go down as I had a certain amount of evidence to give: and I had been watching the race on a point of the course and had seen the runners three times and the man who was alleged to have done the pacing, a Company Sergeant Major, had been with me for quite a time and I could at any rate answer for a considerable fraction of the race and I had seen no pacing. So I went down and said so: and other evidence was given to the same effect and the cumulative effect of it all was sufficient to acquit our men. And so we are already nine points to the good and hope to be alright tomorrow.

On Sunday we were asked to send two officers to the front: the news came in just as we went on church parade and the Adjutant called for officers. He then told us what was wanted and that only subalterns could be spared: and then he asked for volunteers. There were only two subalterns on parade besides myself and we were not quite ready to say yes on such a sudden request. So it was left until we returned from parade. I thought it over during the service and had made up my mind I was ready to go: but we heard when we came back two names had already been sent. I did not feel prepared to say at once that I was ready to go to a battalion where I did not know any of the men and only the officers that have gone from us: and none of those did I know very well. I have made many friends among the officers and I know the men and their various abilities and characteristics and have become part of the battalion by this time and so I am not anxious to go to another unit where I shall be a complete stranger. However, if more are required and I am put down to go, I shall make the best of it.

Wednesday evening.

Today we have had a change in the weather: last night it rained all night up to 8 o'clock this morning. The rain was very heavy and wind got up too: and it was so thick that it came through the Mess tent almost everywhere and while sitting there it was almost impossible to keep out of the wet. But my tent kept beautifully dry and with the door flaps closed it was quite dry: and I was very comfortable and warm all night ...

There is really very little news to give you as day after day passes in camp without anything very distinctive happening. Of course everyone here was very delighted with the victories in France[5] and everyone has looked anxiously and expectantly for the morning and evening papers to see what there is fresh. It may be that the 1st line battalion of the Worcesters were in it as they were near La Bassee[6] but we do not yet quite know. We first heard the news on Sunday night here. One of the sergeants came and spoke to one of our officers and gave the piece of news along with his business. We all scoffed and put it down as a Sunday newspaper lie but next morning we found the official account was almost the same as the sergeant's version and as I say we were all immensely delighted. Our C.O. knew something was coming off during the week and had been waiting for it eagerly and of course he was none the less pleased on that account.

One of our officers here has been 7 months at the front in the Honourable Artillery Company: they landed at St Nazarre on 1st September last year and he was with them until April. He does not speak very much about what he has seen and experienced but occasionally he will talk about it ...

Invermay[7]
Highlands Avenue
Brentwood
[Postmarked 7th November 1915]

Dear Mother

I am now comfortably installed in Brentwood after one or two little adventures. The train I took from Bristol was late and so I was unable to catch the train to Brentwood I had expected but I caught one a little bit later at 7.20 and got to Brentwood a little after 8 o'clock.

As I crossed town I was startled to see on the evening papers that Lord Kitchener had resigned[8] but as I went on I saw that the later papers denied that and as you know now, though he has not yet actually resigned, he will do so before long, it is expected. Whatever he is doing we are glad to know that he has not resigned because of any difference in the Cabinet but because he is taking some important work elsewhere. What the work is I do not know though some of the papers hint he is going to Paris to organise a General Staff there consisting of French and English officers though others suggest he is going to the East to inspect and take command of the armies there and conduct the operations. But we will see.

I arrived in Brentwood about 8.10 and set about finding out where the Battalion Headquarters were. No one at the station knew and I had considerable difficulty in finding out but I managed to discover bit by bit where they were and it was nearly 9 o'clock before I got there. I went in and reported and found out where my Captain was billeted. I looked him up and found him out but as he has a house with five other officers I was able to see them and they offered to put me up there for the night in the place of one who was away on a course. I accepted this offer and had a bed and breakfast with them and then I saw the billeting officer and he took me to my billet. I went there and made arrangements and then we had a parade which I took. After lunch I went out with some other officers who were going to have some practice at hockey. I was lent a stick and though I was in uniform I took part, taking off my coat and belt. Of course I got frightfully hot and as it was my first attempt I felt rather done after a bit. I was very glad however and it helped to pass the afternoon away. Afterwards I went and looked round the town and made one or two purchases.

Captain Boucher has gone on leave this weekend and will be back tomorrow night. So for the time being I am in charge of the company. He left me directions as to what he wanted done but I was left some discretion. So today I have had to think over what I would do for tomorrow and I have now a programme made up ready for tomorrow. He will be back tomorrow night and then of course I shall be relieved. But we have not much to do and I think I shall be able to get on alright. It is the first time almost I have had to decide on the training for the other times I have been in charge we have had definite orders and I have only to see that they are carried out.

I am in my billet now: it seems a very comfortable house something of the sort of house you meet in New Clifton[9], those of the better sort I mean. I have not a sitting room to myself but there is a fireplace in the hall with a table and seats and a screen so as to be almost a little room, and there I can smoke and work and do as I please. It will be very comfortable and I ought to be able to work there quite well. And I am told I can entertain my friends there if I wish. The family consists of a husband and wife and two daughters, one just grown up and the other not quite so, named Robertson.[10] In the back there is a tennis court and the front is the road. It is a fairly pretty neighbourhood with the country close round but there is a factory not far away which is making munitions. I am only about 5 minutes away from the Company and the Battalion Headquarters: so that I shall have no trouble to keep in touch with all that is going on.

The Company is billeted in a school called the Highwood Schools.[11] These schools are a series of buildings in a large ground and we use four buildings as barrack rooms for platoons and then another building as a Mess Room for the men and another room in the same building as the Sergeants' Mess. And in the middle of those four buildings is the house where the Captain and five other officers are billeted.

Altogether the Company is splendidly billeted and we have all the men together. So we can do much more with them than the other companies who are all scattered and A Company ought to be the best and smartest and most disciplined of the whole battalion. We have now in the Company a full complement of officers: and we can begin to get to work. I am the second senior but how the arrangements will be made if any I do not know.

I hardly know Brentwood yet but it is a bigger place than I thought. There is the whole of our Brigade here and the Brigadier has taken a big house here quite close to us less than five minutes walk away and next door to our Battalion Orderly Room. There are besides ourselves a number of Army Cyclists in Brentwood whose Headquarters are farther down our road: and then there is Warley Barracks[12] just outside the town where are a battalion of Irish Guards with the Earl of Kerry in command. So that you see there are plenty of troops in the town. There are no South Africans here yet but I have seen one or two men in the town probably visiting relatives ...

Maldon I thought was dark enough and London too but Brentwood beats them both at night. Every window has to be closed, blinds drawn down and curtains pulled across. The street lamps are not lighted and it takes some little time to move about at night as one runs into people before one sees them unless one is very careful ...

I trust you are all quite well since I left you. I shall want to be kept fully informed of all Bristol news and how Harold and Walter are both doing. I shall look forward to hear especially of Walter and his firm and what changes are being made and how they will affect Walter. I shall want to hear too about the recruiting canvass[13] and what is being done in Bristol and what happens about Harold and Walter ...


Invermay

[Postmarked 15th November 1915]

Dear Mother

There is very little news about here and I hardly suppose I shall have much to tell you all the winter as we shall go on training steadily in the barrack rooms and do nothing very big or important ...

During the next six weeks I am to have a special job. I am to help the Machine Gun Officer, Mr Goodwin, in training the whole of the battalion in the Machine Gun. We are to have them in batches of 56 at a time and have each batch for ten days and we are to train them to have a fair knowledge of machine gun work. It is very interesting and of course I shall learn a lot and at times too I am to have the Machine Gun Section so that when it is done I ought to have myself a very good knowledge of Machine Gun tactics and drill and everything else. Besides that the guns we are to get will be the Vickers Light Gun[14]: this was the gun I was trained on at Bisley while the Machine Gun officer himself had the Maxim. So I shall have a bit more work there when they come. Of course there is not much difference and the differences can be soon learnt. Still it is lucky I know the gun. So you see I am getting some responsible work to do ...

Last night I went to see my Captain and found Spreat who had been to the front talking of some of his experiences. He does not often talk about them so I was very glad to listen. He told us his battalion of the H.A.C. went through Bailleul[15] eight days after the Germans had occupied the town. Numbers of the women there were mad from what they had suffered from the Germans. He told us too that when they were going through a village one of their men noticed that the hands of the clock were pointed to a certain hour. This clock was in a church tower and this tower was the only building left standing. They were caught by shrapnel on the road just after and when they returned they noticed the hands of this clock were pointing to an entirely different hour. Later the tower was searched and they found the Mayor of the town hidden up there and in this way by moving the hands he had been signalling to the Germans that troops were passing below. Another time they had been in the trenches all day and had been heavily shelled. At night some platoons of the Royal Scots were moved into the trenches to support them. One of them told Spreat to lie down in the bottom of the trench and rest and as the trench was wet he went back to get some straw from a rick 200 yds behind the trenches. When he came back he said there was a dead German behind the rick. During the day a lot of sniping had been going on from behind and the H.A.C. had lost men by it: but one of them had thought he had seen the sniper up this rick and fired and got him because the sniping ceased and so at night it had been proved true because there was this dead German. The Germans you know when they were driven back in North France left behind a lot of men with unlimited ammunition for this purpose: to hide and snipe troops as they passed and this was one of them.

I was very interested about Harold and Walter. I presume now their position has been made quite plain. If not they had better see about it because I feel sure conscription will be here before long: it is getting clearer every day. You can console Walter I think quite well. He need not worry because munitions are more important than men almost. Our men are undoubtedly better than the Germans and all we want now is abundance of all kinds of munitions to beat them. So the man in the factory is as good as the man in the trench ...

[Probably 22nd November 1915]

Dear Mother

I have had a very busy week doing routine work but I handed over this morning to another man and he carries on and I shall get a rest for a week or so. That must be my excuse for not writing to Walter for his birthday.[16] Let me wish him many happy returns now. As a matter of fact I have had so much to think about this week that I had forgotten it though I made a mental note of it at the beginning of the week ...

I am now Second-In-Command of the Company and have a lot more work to do in the Company Office. I have a lot of the correspondence to see to and am responsible to the Captain for the Messing of the men, the pay and the finance of the Company and the kit and equipment. This is new work to me and is what Jack Webb has to do. Of course it is a step up and besides that I get a greater part of the training of the Company. If my Captain decides to keep me at it I ought to be promoted before long: and I am hoping it will come off ...

We are besides constantly losing men who have been taken for munition work and so we are getting less and less each week: but the rumours continue that we are to be made up to strength before long but I am unable to say more as no one knows. I had a card from Leslie this morning: he says he is quite well and will be writing soon. I wrote to him last Sunday and my letter has reached him ...

I have been to Brentwood Church tonight: we had no church parade this morning as only two companies go each week and it was our turn last week. Brentwood Church is very high quite like All Saints Clifton.[17] We have a procession sometimes but there was none tonight. The service is of course the usual Evensong. The preacher tonight partly amused and partly annoyed me: he was not a very good preacher. He did amuse me however, by saying 'five biscuits and two sardines' instead of 'five loaves and two fishes'. The music is very good and there is a fine organ and choir there. It is less than ten minutes walk from my billet and is quite easy to get at. The church is always crowded in the evening and many officers go. We have chairs not pews just as at All Saints and the chancel is painted very nicely. The lamps however are shaded to throw all the light on the congregation and none to the windows: that is the effect of Zeppelins.

The country round here is very pretty and solely given up to agriculture: it looks very quaint and old-world and there are a lot of windmills[18] about. There is too a lot of game preserving done. I went out for a walk yesterday as hockey was impossible owing to the state of the ground and did the same today. Otherwise I have hardly been farther than from my billet to the schools where the Company is quartered, less than five minutes walk, all the week because I was so busy.

I shall have to be careful what I am writing as we had a list of subjects sent us which ought not to be discussed in letters. This was a confidential War Office letter and though I suppose it does not apply very much to letters written to people in this country one never knows and we were warned it was an offence against the Defence of the Realm Act[19] to talk of certain subjects in correspondence.

There is not much chance of me being home at Christmas I believe. The Colonel is arranging for a good Christmas dinner for the men as they will all be here and if all the men are here so too will be the officers. The Colonel will not naturally allow a public subscription to be made for the men's Christmas dinner but he gave us the hint that if we knew anyone who would subscribe privately we could get any money we could. He wants beef and goose, Christmas pudding, fruits and nuts to be on the table and the men are to have a thorough good feed ...


Brentwood
[Postmarked 6th December 1915]

Dear Mother

This week has passed very much the same as last but there have been one or two interesting little incidents. It has been very wet since Friday but the earlier part of the week was fine ...

This week we have had a real machine gun: it belongs to the Brigade and it is given to battalions in turn and it was our turn this week. We took it on Tuesday and we return it again on Tuesday: we give it to the 8th Worcesters and got it from the 6th Gloucesters. Jack Langford is the MGO (ie. Machine Gun Officer) of the 6th Gloucesters: and he handed it over to us. The gun we have is a Maxim: the one I learnt at Bisley was a Vickers but the differences are not very great and of course most of the work is exactly the same.

Besides this we have a good big bombing class started and other work is going on. We have bayonet fighting and entrenching each week and there is a big musketry class for recruits. This of course is private information for yourselves. I believe I should be liable to prosecution under the Defence of the Realm Act if necessary for making known these facts. But you see we are really working on what will be useful to know. We are not going in for anything like attack practices which are rather a washout nowadays but it is all trench warfare for us. Even musketry is practically useless in the trenches because no one ever gets a chance to shoot. No one is so foolish as to poke his head above the trench so that no one can shoot. What is useful is Machine Gunnery and Bombing and these we are busy on now ...

The other day, on Thursday to be precise, an aeroplane passed over Brentwood, circled round and then began to descend in spirals. I was Orderly Officer that day and was at the issue of rations between 4 o'clock and 4.30 when it happened. Then we saw it glide to earth. Well it was reported to me as Orderly Officer that it had landed and I reported it to the Adjutant. It was obviously some distance off where it had landed and so we took no further notice of it. But later in the evening we were called on to furnish a guard for it: I was not at Headquarters that evening and so I knew nothing of it at the time though all these things are supposed to be in my care. However, I came in later and heard about it by accident. I tried to find out where it had fallen but no one knew. I intended to visit it that night as I ought to but as no one could tell me I had to give it up as it was hopeless to look for it on a dark night like that night was. But next morning I got up a bit earlier and went to try to find it before breakfast. After many enquiries I did find it after wandering round a lot: and I went to the guard. Nothing had happened during the night but it was very cold and damp though it did not rain. It was not a very big machine though a labourer whom I asked where it was told me it was 'a terrible big thing'. It had come down in a field of stubble between two coppices. I had a good look at it. It was painted blue grey and had rings painted on the wings: the outer ring was red, the next white and the inner which was a small circle was blue. This is the marking of British aeroplanes. Then again on the tail were two plates of metal, these painted likewise in red, white and blue. I was interested to notice that some alterations had been made since I was last able to examine one from near at hand at Filton.[20] The planes are no longer made of canvas but of thin sheets of tin corrugated. The upper plane too was longer than the lower which was cut short at both sides. The propeller was of thick strong wood and it was built to carry two with two seats one directly behind the other. The pilot who was in front was evidently meant to look out from beneath the upper plane but the observer who was directly behind him from above it. There was a little teddy bear fastened to the right side of the car as a mascot. On the tail was a number 5065: so that if they are numbered consecutively this gives you some idea of the number of machines we have in the country. This again is information which might be of use to the enemy so that you had better not let this letter get about ...

On the evening I had tea with a party of officers who are billeted together in the schools. The Adjutant was there too and we talked about various things. The Adjutant told us how he had learned to cook returns at the Brigade office. Stevenson is the Staff Captain who has to see to the returns sent in and Capt Vigers is the Adjutant of the 8th Worcesters. Well the Brigadier had called for a return of men trained in various branches of war. Vigers brought in the return of the 8th Worcesters and the Brigadier looked at it. Then happened as follows. The Brigadier on looking at it noticed only five men trained in bombing. So he said, 'What only five men trained in bombing! I can't send that into Division: I shall look ridiculous after telling them what we have been doing. Stevenson add a 0 to that. That's about right, isn't it, Vigers?' 'Yes, Sir.' I was very much amused at that for Sir John Barnsley a prominent Weslyan like he is ...

You ask me if there is not another church in Brentwood I can go to. There is but it is Roman Catholic and there is no Low Church close: the nearest is three miles or more away and on these dark nights it would take too long to get there. That is at Warley[21] and there is no other church in Brentwood itself. The Roman Catholics are very strong around here. Lord Petre and the Petre family are Roman Catholics[22] and there is a convent here where the little Belgian Prince is being educated. But there is no nearer Low Church ...


Brentwood
[dated 12th December 1915]

Dear Mother
One day last week, Wednesday I had a day out in the air: we had to send a party to dig trenches on the London defences[23] and we had to take lunch. It was just an hour's march to get to the farm where we had to draw tools and then we had to cross a field to the trenches ... I was very much interested to observe how the trenches were sited and how the different features of the ground were treated: particularly a long bare ridge which ran right into the line of trenches. When we got there we found part of the trenches which was only half dug almost full of water: other parts which had been finished were fairly dry as the drains were

working well and carrying off all the water. But even then the trenches would have been unpleasant places to live in as the wind would have been very bad. One of our first jobs was to make a drain for the half dug trenches so that the water would run off and try and cut a path for the water, and of course we had a lot of baling out to do. However in spite of it all the men seemed very cheerful and laughed and joked and we got along quite alright. The Civil Engineer in charge said that our Worcestershire lads always worked well on the trenches and he gave us a very good name. Of course he is in charge permanently and we get our orders from him ... At times I think I could have filled a flowerpot with the mud from off my boots. It was a heavy sticky clay: the worst possible stuff for trenches as it holds the wet and is liable to fall in with rain and crumbles in dry weather.

I am glad to hear Walter has joined Lord Derby's reserve[24]: and I hope he will find everything comfortable though I do not expect he will be called on for sometime if his sight is so bad. Though the eyesight test is suspended now it will be revived when the groups are called up I have no doubt because the sight is very important in war, almost the most important physical qualification of the lot: and of course the great majority of the men enrolled will be first class, up to any standard they may choose to set. What will be done I cannot say of course: but of course the men will have to be taken gradually so that they all can be absorbed. The difficulty now will not be the equipping but the training of the new recruits.

One of our officers went to Ilford on Friday to attest 1000 recruits and again yesterday when probably the number would have grown to 2000. I hope we get a share of these Lord Derby's recruits. Our own recruiting party which has returned to us this week has secured 100 men ...


Brentwood
[Postmarked 20th December 1915]

Dear Mother

Well we have had the same routine as usual this week: but the weather has been wet again. However it has cleared up wonderfully today and we have a nice bright sunny day for our Sunday. We have gone on the same way and there have been no changes in any way in the battalion.

One day we had a trench catapult here for throwing bombs: it belongs to the Brigade and is handed over to each battalion in turn for instruction and practice. We had it on Wednesday I think and our bombing class was out on the Alarm Post with it throwing bombs at a mark they had set up. I watched it for a time and was very interested. It is made of wood and can be set up against the parapet of a trench and it will throw bombs for about 300 yds. The strands are made of elastic rubber and the machine is wound up with a handle and then released. The bombs are put in a little cradle and are thrown out when the elastic is released. The fuse of the bomb is lighted just before the machine is released. Our men were practising with dummy bombs and they were fairly successful though I did not see them hit the mark. Another day they were practising throwing bombs by hand ...

I discover I have run out of paper so I must write on the two sides.

We are to have a good Christmas here if possible: and I am faced with the problem of having to eat two Christmas dinners. Here at my billet they treat Christmas like Sunday and have the dinner at mid-day: and on the night there is to be a dinner for the officers at the White Hart Hotel [25] and the married officers will bring their wives and children. So you see I shall have to eat two dinners. Besides that the Colonel has arranged for a thorough good old-fashioned Christmas dinner for the men which everyone will have to attend and the officers will visit it to wish the men

A trench catapult designed to launch a grenade into the enemy's trenches. In the background are 'knife rests', ready-made barbed-wire obstacles to block roads

good cheer. In the evening besides there is to be an entertainment at the Drill Hall and we shall leave it to go to our own dinner. There may be a Brigade Church Parade in the morning: at any rate there will be on the Sunday, the day afterwards. So you see we shall have a busy Christmas and I ought to have a very good time. Of course I should prefer to be home as you know but still this is a sacrifice I must make for King and country and I shall be thinking of you a lot during this coming week. I am sending the enclosed cheque as my contribution towards Christmas and I want you to use it so as to have a Christmas of the usual kind. I am afraid there will be many poor Christmases in England this year and all over the world and I am glad I can do something to cheer you at least. I will leave the money in your hands to be used as you think best in providing for Christmas or to purchase Christmas presents for you at home.

I will try to write to Leslie, Wilfrid, Jack Webb and others this week as a Christmas greeting but I expect I shall be busy during the week. The Colonel wants the houses occupied by our Company to be decorated for Christmas and I shall have to be busy to see to the house I have to look after. I have made some arrangements already with my Sergeant and I suppose we shall spend Christmas Eve putting it up. The people I am billeted with here have lent me some things which will be a help ...


Brentwood
[Late December 1915]

Dear Mother

I have had a full week as you would naturally expect in Christmas week and I have lots to tell you.

First of all I have been given full charge of the Reserve Section of Machine Gunners and I have to train them myself: I am solely and entirely responsible for them. I am very glad to have a little job of my own at last as I have a chance of training according to my own ideas.

Next as I think I have told you on Monday I went to town to do some shopping and buy one or two presents. I bought one or two books for myself, a new hat badge, some buttons which I am going to distribute, a box of chocolates for Heybridge Hall and one for the billet here. I saw Edwards and had a talk with him, went in at the main entrance and had to fill in a pink form stating my business and whom I wished to see: and then a Boy Scout was told where to take me and I went off. I tramped miles through the corridors and went up a lift and then found out the department had been moved out of the buildings: so I came down under the guidance of the same Boy Scout and was shown out having received a paper telling me where to go but it was tea time and so I had tea first and set out to see Edwards afterwards.

I found him ensconced in a little room at the National Portrait Gallery and had quite a nice little chat with him. He told me he was to have four days leave at Christmas and that he was still busy and had all sorts of people come to see him from Countesses downwards. After chatting with him I went out to dinner.

When I went to lunch that morning I asked permission of the C.O. to go to town which he gave me. When I went out in the afternoon he asked me which train I meant to catch and I told him and he said he meant to go by the same. So I joined him on the station and in the train he asked me to dine with him and I of course accepted. Then he told me to meet him at the United Services Club: to which I went after I had seen Edwards. I found him there alright and we chatted a bit before dinner and then he showed me round the club. All the walls are covered with pictures of famous soldiers and sailors, Nelson, Wellington, Lord Gough, the Duke of Cambridge, Abercrombie and a host of others including Sir John Moore with his sword hung below the picture. We had dinner in the dining room and he pointed out to me various men sitting down: of course you know it is the club to which most of the service men belong and Sir John French[26] had been there only the day before. The Colonel told me a good deal about the generals who are commanding us now, Generals Townshend, Sir John Nixon, General Birdwood, Sir Douglas Haig and many others and also I heard a good deal of life in India. He enquired what I intended to be and I told him I had intended to go into the Indian Civil Service[27] and of course as an old Anglo-Indian he was very interested. He told me a good deal about Army life and how very happy it was in India but the Civil Service he said was the more lucrative of the two and gave the better opportunities of becoming comfortable. We left the club just before nine o'clock and took a bus to the station, caught the train with plenty of time to spare and got back home just before eleven o'clock: we walked up from the station together as the C.O.'s billet is just a little nearer Headquarters than myself. I had a very interesting and enjoyable time altogether and of course I was very glad to see something of the seats of the mighty. Incidentally I heard a good deal about Mr & Mrs Asquith.[28]

You will want to know of course how I spent Christmas. Well, Christmas was a very merry and a very busy time for all here. I got up early on Christmas Day at 6 o'clock and dressed carefully and went out to the early service at 7 o'clock at the church with the girl from this billet who was the only one to go. The church was fairly full and there must have been 400 people there including a lot of officers. We were out before 8 o'clock as there was another service there to which the C.O. went. Then I came back and had breakfast and went on church parade at 8.45 and was in church again at 9.10. We came back however by ten o'clock and then I had to see to one or two things for the dinner at the Drill Hall. I came back to the schools and had to show Miss Baker round the buildings which the men had decorated with flags, papers and green stuff. Miss Baker went into each room (by the way, Miss Baker is the Matron of the schools) and I had to show her round. The Captain had promised a prize to the best room and the Colonel was to judge. As the Colonel did not come when expected I went with Goodwin the Machine Gun Officer whose men are billeted here to ask him to come. He awarded the prize to one of the rooms in my cottage at the schools. Other prizes were also given, another of which came to my house. I was very pleased though I had nothing to do with it beyond making some arrangements: the men did all the decorations themselves and did them extremely well too …

Then I came back to my billet and had some dinner, it was the Christmas dinner here: and I had to go at once afterwards and fall in the company for their Christmas dinner and march them to the Drill Hall where they were to have it. The Brigadier and the Colonel and all the officers in Brentwood were present: and when all were seated the officers went on to the platform, the Brigadier said a few words and the Colonel too and then we drank the health of the battalion. After that we left the Hall as soon as the dinner was fairly commenced. I came back and showed the people here the decorations in the schools and then until teatime I was able to have a rest. After tea at 6 o'clock there was an entertainment in the Drill Hall which the Brigadier and officers attended. I took the girl from the billet here, Miss Robinson and brought her back. The entertainment was very good: it was provided by Captains Grainger and Green and it included a ventriloquist, a girl who sang and two men and besides one of our officers sang twice; the men appreciated the ventriloquist very much and the applause was very vigorous. Directly it was finished we went down to the White Hart Hotel and had our own dinner. The officers brought their wives and there were one or two other friends including Miss Baker, the Matron of the Schools. We had a very good dinner of six courses, dessert and coffee and when it was done we had music chiefly songs, one or two recitations. It was a very jolly affair and was over quite early. I was back in my billet just after 11 o'clock and into bed before midnight. So you see I had a busy Christmas though a very enjoyable one ...

Please thank Miss Green very much for her little present: and thank you very much for yours. It is proving very welcome as I have to be out before breakfast this week and then the chocolate comes in useful.

Brentwood
[Probably early January 1916]

Dear Mother

I owe you the news of a fortnight in this letter and I am very sorry I have not written before but I have had one of the busiest times I have had since I joined the battalion. I have been in charge of the Company for nearly a week now and I have been in command of the Machine Gun Section for a week but the Machine Gun Officer is now back and I have handed over. Besides these I have had a week at my own little job of the Reserve Machine Gun Section ...

So I am the 'Officer Commanding A Company' for four weeks and am consequently entitled to give punishments, be responsible for the discipline, training, feeding, clothing, paying and welfare of nearly 140 N.C.O.s and men during that period. Besides that I am informed we are to have two hundred or two fifty Derby recruits[29] within a fortnight and I shall have to make arrangements I dare say with regard to their Messing and quartering. So you see I have a fairly big job on for the next weeks ...

Tomorrow we are doing night work for the first time since we have been in Brentwood: these winter evenings of course give us a chance of doing this work without being late: tomorrow for instance we shall be out from 6.30 to 8.30pm. I am surprised we have not done any before now. We are getting ready for proceeding overseas now: but of course we do not know where we shall go or when. However, it is said we are to go in March: but if we have 200 or 250 of Lord Derby's men it will hardly be possible to take them abroad in March as they cannot be trained so quickly. They are to come somewhere about Jan 20th but that would only give us six or eight weeks to train them and that of course is insufficient. It would mean nearly one man out of every three would be untrained and we would be almost useless with such a large proportion of recruits. But it is one of the signs that we are getting ready: it is almost the first essential for us to be made up to strength. We have had most of the equipment now which we ought to have but the important things, rifles, machine guns and rangetakers are yet to appear. However a letter has arrived promising to supply some machine guns to the Central Force within six weeks or two months so that we may hope to have one soon: an enquiry has been sent asking if we have any range takers too. But we have heard nothing about rifles though rumours as to their probable advent are about but we have seen nothing of them yet. However by all accounts we are not to be in England much longer: in fact the Brigadier said so plainly at the Christmas dinner. But whether these plans will have been in any way postponed because of Lord Derby's recruits I cannot say. Whether we shall stay here much longer I do not know either but it seems to be anticipated that we shall go to Aldershot or Salisbury Plain to finish our training. In fact we must go because we shall have to fire a musketry course before we go and there is nowhere to do it at Brentwood ...

Thank you very much for your letters: the other two were bills, one from Matthew Todd Ltd and the other from Gordon L Kinnersley.[30] I have also sent for my pass-book this week: and you will be pleased to know my balance has been going up slowly all the time though it has stayed between £50 and £60 ever since July. Of course it has been rather expensive for me ever since I left Maldon as I have been going about a lot and the two courses at Bisley were both fairly expensive: then of course there was my journey home and back here but since I have been here I have not spent much except for Christmas. And this month's pay and expenditure ought about to balance or leave me on the right side in spite of the two bills I have referred to. But before we leave England I shall have to buy some larger articles such as a revolver and compass and several small things before I shall be ready. However, when all is said and done I shall have saved well out of my year's pay and if I get promotion it will be easier for me still. So you need have no doubts as to this side of my affairs and of course on service it will be almost impossible to spend money at all.[31] So you can be quite easy about this: I am very thankful that all is working out so well: in fact I am in a better position than I have ever been ...

Thank you very much for your letters and your enquiries but I leave it entirely to you though a khaki pocket handkerchief is the only thing I can suggest as all my white ones will have to be sent home. I shall be glad to hear of Walter and Harold. I have been thinking very much about Harold under the new Compulsion Bill.[32] And I should like to know what he is doing or intends to do: and I hope he is not at all alarmed over it ...

Brentwood
[Postmarked 17th January 1916]

Dear Mother

This week has passed very quickly, very much like all the rest and there is not very much to tell you about. But I have been busy all the time all the same ...

An order has come from the Brigade that every officer must be able to ride and ride well. So on Thursday I thought I would have my first lesson. I went down to the transport stables and a horse was got out for me and I managed to get on alright and got him to travel up a track for a few yards until he got into an open space. I was told this animal was quiet and would be easy to ride: so I was going out for a ride with another man if all went well. But when I got to this open space things began to go wrong. The beast would not go where I wanted him to: I tried to make him by turning his head in the right direction but he would merely spin round. He stopped dead, stood still a moment and then jumped up and repeated that once or twice. Then he started off at a good pace and suddenly swung round. I lost a stirrup and nearly came off but saved myself. After a bit he started off hard again but I pulled up and after that he did not try to get rid of me. I got off and had a rest and got on again after one of the drivers had tried him and still he would not go where I wanted him. After that the Transport Officer came out and gave me a few minutes lesson and then I got off and he was put away and we came back to Headquarters for an officers' meeting. I was very stiff next day and had to do all the marching and so on Saturday I was more stiff still, in fact I was so stiff I could hardly move. However, I learnt something and I am glad to think I managed to stick on though it was in no very orthodox manner. The beast certainly did all he knew to get me off. I have made up my mind to learn to ride at once as it is necessary and of course there is the order: besides that I want to do so myself.

This coming week will be even busier for me. We are to have 324 recruits in this battalion, 92 of whom are coming to 'A' Company. I shall have to arrange for their billeting, their feeding and their accommodation. I have had to do some of it today but it will be a difficult piece of work and will require a lot of organisation. Another company 'C' Company is coming in to the schools and I shall have to make a lot of arrangements with the Captain of that company. I am told that the men we are to have, have all had a month's training at least but they do not know what discipline means and they have been accustomed to do as they like. So we shall have a pretty thick time of it and it will require firmness and resolution to lick them into shape. However, I shall be severe with them from the start and not let them have too much rope as this will only mean trouble in the end. It is far better to get the thing done with at once and let them see that they cannot do as they like with us whatever they might have done before. You see I am coming in for some responsible work now: I have been in charge of the Company for nearly a fortnight and will be for another at least and all this comes into my sphere as Company Commander.

I hear that we are likely to move from Brentwood in a month and go to Salisbury Plain for twelve weeks to finish off our training before going abroad. But nothing is yet known officially about it though. I feel certain it is true as this is always done. I was very glad of Walter's letter and shall await eagerly the news of what he is to do when called up. And I am glad too to hear that Harold's position is so good under the new Bill ...


Brentwood
[Probably late January 1916]

Dear Mother

I was so busy last week and so tired on Sunday that I was unable to write to you but I am now trying to get this letter finished tonight. The draft arrived last week and I have had a very busy and trying time to make all the arrangements necessary for quartering, equipping and messing the men. We had 92 posted to our Company and that has very nearly doubled our strength so that you can see we had a big job to absorb them. They all came from the 3rd line units of our regiments and all the Brigade has had drafts just as ourselves though of course the numbers varied with the varying strength of the different battalions. We had 324 men in all and this makes up the strength of our battalion to about 850. They seem a fairly good lot though some of them are quite unfit: in fact I have one man who is suffering from consumption who is so bad that the doctor says he may drop dead at any minute. Besides him I have some others who will be totally unfit for service. Then they have had no discipline at all and we have got to get them into shape. Some have had quite a lot of training while others have only joined about three or four weeks: so you can see we shall have a lot of work to get them ready for the front. I suppose this will put us back at least a couple of months and for that time we shall stay in England. When we leave Brentwood it is said we shall go to Salisbury Plain but it is quite uncertain when we are to move and we have no idea but it does not seem so near now as it did at Christmas. But we are all getting ready and today all the officers were medically examined but with what results we have not yet heard ...

Thank you very much for the parcel you sent me: I was very pleased with so many handkerchiefs and the chocolate. The chocolate I have got rid of already: in fact the cake of Cadbury's went in one morning. I took it out on a route march because I had not had much time for breakfast and so expected to feel hungry but the chocolate went chiefly to hungry subalterns who managed to take away it all. One man particularly had a good lot: he had been out like myself and had even less time and less breakfast than I: and he was able to get through half the amount. He must have been hungry I know because I was quite hungry enough.

Last week on Wednesday I think it was, I had my first promotion and am now Lieutenant instead of 2nd Lieutenant with two stars on my arm instead of one. Captain Grainger was made Major, dated September 29th; Capt Green, Major also but dated December 14th; and 2nd Lieutenants Hemingway, Spreat and myself Lieutenant and dated September 15th. I am senior to Spreat but junior to Hemingway. Being dated back to September 15th means that I get back pay to that date: now I get 8/6d a day instead of 7/6d and I shall draw an extra shilling for every day since Sept 15th. It works out to over £6. And of course I get seniority to that date: I am therefore senior to many lieutenants in the Brigade who were gazetted before me because they were dated on the days they were gazetted or slightly back: but you see I am dated back 4 months and more. The Lieutenants who were gazetted while we were at Epping were dated September 14: so I am only one day junior to men who had six or seven months more service than I. But it will work out fairly equally I expect because while they will become Captains fairly quickly we shall have to wait some time for it ...

My servant has left me during the week: he was found unfit and sent to the Provisional Battalion at Clacton for Home Service. I was very sorry as I liked him very much. He too was very sorry as he wanted to be out in France and he liked everyone so much in the Battalion. But he was only getting worse with us and he had lost nearly a stone in weight so that it was best for him that he did not come. He had been a miner and the fire damp in the mines, a poisonous gas, had got into his system so that he was constantly getting headaches. He was a very good servant, and a very nice man: quiet but with as much pluck as you could wish: he had never fallen out on a march though a march always gave him a violent headache. So you see he was too good a man to lose. I have a new servant but I cannot quite say how he will turn out. My last servant Guest has been the only servant I have liked yet and he was my fourth. My new does his work well but I don't think he will do more than he can help and he is rather faint-hearted. I am going to send my watch home for repairs as I cannot get them done satisfactorily here so you may expect it soon ...

Brentwood
[Probably mid February 1916]

Dear Mother

I have had quite a lot of interesting news to tell you that has happened to me since I last wrote. I think I had best start with last Monday.

I went up to town on Monday because I broke my glasses on Saturday and was unable to get repairs in Brentwood. As I had plenty of time to spare in town I determined I go and call on your cousin Lucy Skinner.[33] I found Portland Place without much trouble although I went round farther than I need have done: then I discovered Devonshire Street and then I looked for 29. As the street was numbered rather curiously I had a little trouble in finding No. 29 but I did so and rang the bell and asked for Miss Skinner. The maid replied she had left nearly two years but she could get the address for me. So I went in and a lady came dressed as a nurse and wrote it down for me and I am enclosing it. She said she had not heard from Miss Skinner since September but as she was asked to forward letters to address enclosed she presumes she is there still. I went to have tea then and then I had my glasses seen to and then I looked Edwards up. I had quite a long chat with him and I suggested he should bring a team down to play hockey against us at Brentwood. This has now been arranged and they will be coming down the last Saturday in February. He told me that news of Zeppelins had arrived and that if I stayed late I should not be able to get a train but as I had no intention of being late I did not feel alarmed.

I left him and made my way back to the Liverpool St. to find sure enough the station closed and the train service stopped. As there was no chance of getting a train for some time I went back to get some dinner: I found a place fairly close and spent an hour at dinner and then I returned to the station which was still closed. I waited for twenty minutes and was then thinking of trying to find a taxi to take me back to Brentwood when I heard that the lights had been put up again on the Metropolitan and so I waited and in a minute or two I heard an engine whistle and about ten o'clock the station was opened. It took me another hour to find a train to Brentwood and then it took the train an hour to get to Brentwood: I had to stand up in a luggage van all the way back. I must say that the prospect of an air raid did not seem to make the slightest difference to London: things were all as usual, buses, taxis, tubes and cabs were all running; the train service was stopped because it is known the Zeps have followed the trains on various occasions. At Liverpool St. there were crowds and about a quarter of an hour after the station was opened the place was packed, people were coming up from the tubes I suppose. There were a lot of soldiers coming back from leave who were anxious about their passes which were all made out for 9 o'clock or so: and of course there were several bad-tempered old gentlemen on the platform. However, as we know now the Zeps were never very near us: where they were was the district this battalion comes from, Dudley, Kidderminster, Stourport, Tipton and so on, the Black Country. Bombs were dropped on the suburbs of Birmingham and the airships crossed the city but dropped no bombs except in the suburbs. Jack Langford and one of our officers, Goodwin, were in Birmingham visiting the B.S.A. works to inspect the manufacture of machine guns: Major Green too was on leave and he relates how he swarmed up two lamposts (the first time for many years, he says) to douse the lights in front of his house at Stourport. Of course, the men are greatly excited over it: one man in my company lost his grandfather, grandmother, mother, father and sister, the whole family by one bomb. I imagine this was the district where the greatest damage and the greatest casualties occurred because from various accounts I have heard I gather a good many lives were lost. Others of ours besides myself had adventures that night but none serious and no Zeppelins came anywhere near London ...

On Friday last we had another little adventure. An officer of the Engineers came down to give us an account of the use of poison gas at the front and the means of protection. It was very interesting indeed and at the end of it he said we were all to test these methods. So we all had to put on gas helmets, even Sir John Barnsley and he made us double about in them for a minute or two: you know the trouble with the gas helmet is you cannot breathe pure air in though means of exhaling through the mouth is provided. So if you have to double, the helmet becomes very hot and of course you must not let air in from elsewhere or you will be poisoned. So the use of these things becomes an art and it certainly requires practice as I was most uncomfortable in mine. After doubling about we had to go into a chamber where chlorine was being made and chlorine is the gas used by the Germans. Enough chlorine was being produced to kill anyone in five minutes when the door was shut and we went in in batches and stayed there in the closed room for five minutes. There were no casualties. After that we took off our masks and went in another room where another gas was being made. This was tear-producing stuff, the stuff put into the 'lacrimatory shells' etc. which you see mentioned in the paper. After being there two minutes the eyes began to smart and water and every one cleared out: if continued it would have caused temporary blindness but it has no after effects. Then we went home. So you may rest in peace and be sure as long as I have my helmet on I shall not be gassed ...

I have spent £2.16 on a revolver getting it from the Government at a cheap price. It arrived on Friday week and I like it very much: it is a Colt pattern and of course takes service ammunition. I have not fired with it yet but hope to make a good shot as the chief point is keeping steady and I am learning that in snapping. I have besides given a cheque for £6.30 for a pair of prismatic fieldglasses which give a much wider field and are stronger than my present pair: besides it is necessary to have a reserve and these things may mean my life one day. Now I am looking out for a good compass which will cost something between 3 and 7 guineas.

I have heard this week that I have been passed as medically fit for active service. Besides that this week I have had to undergo an exam with regard to my knowledge before going to the front. I made some foolish mistakes and had not much time to work up for it but I should think it would be alright though we have not yet heard about it. I was the Senior to undergo and felt very annoyed about it ...

We are going to Salisbury Plain when we leave here: to Perham Down Camp [34] to be more precise. But the date is uncertain, the latest rumour which I heard this morning says March 2nd. Of course Salisbury Plain will be the latest thing before the front where we shall have our final training and fire a course in musketry and have our machine gun and revolver courses each of which I expect I shall have to face. We have had a new General this week: Lord Salisbury left us just before Christmas and Major General Bannatine-Allason who was mentioned in Sir John French's despatches took command: now he has left us in turn and Major General Mackenzie has reported for duty and assumed command. I do not know who he is but he came to Brentwood on Thursday last and looked round the Brigade. I did not see him as I was undergoing the exam I told you about. Why these changes should be made I do not know but I believe General Allason returned from France through sickness and was

Bayonet practice on bags filled with straw, Brentwood 1915

probably unfit for duty. I understand also that Sir John Barnsley and Col Peyton are neither to go out with us as both are over age ... Who we shall have to take us abroad I have not the least idea ...

I suppose now we must be prepared to go out soon, in April I should think: of course to have had such a lot of recruits has put us back several months but they are being pushed on very fast. They have some queer ones amongst them, one who is dying of consumption and another who has such paroxysms of rage that he is to be put in a military institution. This man was brought before me for striking an N.C.O. and the Sgt Major who had seen the affair was so frightened by it that he tried to persuade me not to see him in the room I generally use but in the open: however I did not know of course about it and insisted on seeing him in the Company Office. It turned out alright though I sat directly in front of him and the evidence showed that his temper was very uncertain and that he became very violent when annoyed at anything ...

I shall want to hear what Harold and Walter are doing and what munitions they are making and how they are getting on altogether ...

# SALISBURY PLAIN AT LAST

$A$t the end of February 1916 the battalion moved to Tidworth on Salisbury Plain. They knew it would not be long before they were sent to the front and Stanley's letters once again contain words of comfort and reassurance to his mother. On 20th May he returned home unexpectedly for his last weekend in England. The parish magazine of St Bartholomew's Church later recorded that he had attended a service there with his family just before leaving Bristol on the Sunday evening. On Tuesday 23rd May the battalion left Tidworth for Southampton in two special trains.

Candahar Barracks, Tidworth. There were eight barracks close together, built soon after 1897 and each named after a British victory in India and Afghanistan

Candahar Barracks [1]
S. Tidworth
Salisbury Plain
[Dated 14th March 1916]

Dear Mother

I am feeling much better now but last week I felt rotten. I suppose I had a touch of influenza but another man here gave me a dose of ammoniated quinine [2] and I felt better: I had another the next night and felt worse but the day after I was much better than I had been for a week and am getting still better now ...

I had rather an interesting week last week. I was detailed to attend a bombing course here under a Captain who is instructor of the Salisbury Training Centre: the first two days we had to spend in lectures as the weather was atrocious, sleet and snow and very cold. But the next two days were fine and we spent them in the open in some trenches about a mile away. The first day we practised using dummy bombs, throwing them for a short while and then we took some live ones and threw them under the eye of our instructor. Of course, we had to be careful as the bomb gets broken up into fragments and they travel 100 yds and can do a large amount of damage to anyone whom they hit. But we were in trenches and could take cover if necessary. They were thrown from a trench into a trench but the fun came when a bad shot was made and they fell outside to the ground. After that we were shown how to blow up a trench and of course we took cover from the explosion ...

Another thing we did was to fire the Very pistol: this is the pistol that fires the lights used at night. We all had one show with it: and we had to aim at a trench to make our light fall over or near it to light it up. I put in a fairly good shot. Of course all this was done in daylight so that we could not see the power of the light but there was nothing very difficult or extraordinary about it ...

There was one amusing incident on our first day at a lecture. We were learning the mechanism of the bombs and live bombs were being handed round. One man gave the detonator a knock which set the cap off and lit the fuse. The man behind him saw it and bolted through the door: the rest at that end did likewise while the others in the other side got behind what cover they could or lay flat on the floor expecting the bomb to explode. The instructor who did not know what was up looked anxious and we all thought something was going to happen. But he called us back and then told us the detonator which would be exploded by the fuse was a dummy and the bomb itself was not there as a man took it out with him. So we had a good laugh and set to work again ...

This last Sunday I spent as I have never spent a Sunday before. We had to put off shooting one day as the weather was so bad: so to catch up to our programme we had to fire on Sunday: and I had to go in the butts all day and mark. I was in them from 8 am to 4.15 pm: but got back for a 5 pm tea: then I washed and got clean and went to church in the evening with the Adjutant and Mrs Simpson and another officer named Grove. The Chaplain-General of The Forces Bishop Taylor Smith was preaching and he gave us a very good sermon and I enjoyed it immensely.

I had a chance of coming down to Bristol on Monday but lost it unfortunately. We had a lot of men rejected as medically unfit and these had to be sent to Weston to the 3/7th Worcesters. I was detailed to take charge of the party and conduct them there, but then a notice came that this course I was attending was to continue on Monday so that I had to give it up and another officer took them. I was annoyed especially as it turned out we were only wanted to take a few notes and the whole lecture was less than two hours. I do not know if there will be another chance for me to come down: if there is I shall probably get it but I am very much afraid there will not.

In a fortnight's time I am going to Hayling Island on another course, this time on the Lewis Machine Gun. Hayling Island lies in Portsmouth Harbour and I am looking forward to it as I ought to have a very interesting time. I hear it is a beautiful little place and I shall have to go to Southampton or Portsmouth.

I am sending home two shirts which you will see require mending: I cannot get them decently done here and would like you to do them for me if possible. Please see to them as quickly as you can as I shall be left with only two shirts while they are away ...


c/o Mrs Spraggs
Beversbrook
Church Road
Hayling Island
[Probably 10th April 1916]

Dear Mother

Thank you very much for your letter and the letter enclosed. I am very sorry my letter arrived to you no more than an empty envelope but I remember most distinctly folding the letter up and sending it off. Either the letter must have fallen out in the post or the censor must have retained it. I do not think the latter likely but I did say something about when we expected to go but no more than in previous letters and as there was a good deal of quite harmless stuff I am more inclined to think there was an accident in the post. However I had no news to tell you very much and there was nothing important in it so that it has made no difference to me but I am very sorry you did not receive it because I told you all what I had been doing the week before. I have been in Hayling Island a week and have had quite a good time. The evening we arrived however was terrible: it was blowing heavily and the rain was falling in sheets and everything was as miserable as could be. Next morning when I went up to the School of Musketry from this house, I found a tree lying straight across the road, over which I had to climb as it blocked the road entirely. Next day after being fairly fine but cloudy in the morning it began to blow again but even harder than before and snow came with it but there was nothing like the amount of wet that there was the night before. That was Tuesday, the night of the great gale all over England.[3] Wednesday and Thursday were fine but dull. Friday was better but yesterday and today have been gorgeous days and everything has been beautiful.

We are some little distance from Portsmouth which we can see across the water: as it is, the Island faces right across the English Channel and the East End of the Isle of Wight appears over on the right as one looks out to sea. This is a real island as a narrow channel runs all the way round it which the railway crosses on a causeway. It is very flat but rather pretty: it is cultivated and there are quite a lot of trees about especially firs and pines: the beach is sand and shingles and splendid for bathing because the floor of the sea is sand and there are any amount of bathing huts along the front …

I am in a billet here and able to sleep between sheets once more, a comfort I like very much. There is a man named Bomford on this course from the 8th Worcesters: he and I came down together and are both billeted here …

The course I am on is the Lewis Machine Gun: in the short ten days course we only learn the gun itself and not the way to use it. There is an officer from every battalion in the Brigade down here besides others from another Division. Of course there are other courses going on as well and everywhere there are officers and N.C.O.s billeted …

Yesterday afternoon was a holiday and so Bomford and I decided to go to Portsmouth to see what we could. We walked to the West end of the island

and took the ferry over to Southsea: we had to walk on to the trams and got into Portsmouth that way as Southsea and Portsmouth are continuous. Bomford did a certain amount of shopping then we had tea in the town and went down to the seafront at Southsea. It was not a very pleasant place so after looking about we strolled on and came by accident to the mouth of the docks and harbour, just in time to see two destroyers going out. The 'Victory' was just a little way away and an old sailor offered to take us across in his boat and so we went. We spent half-an-hour in looking over it and then we had to get back to catch our tram and got back quite early. I don't think I had better put in this letter what we heard and all we saw: but at any rate we can tell you about the Victory.

The Victory is quite empty now: but before the War it used to be used as the Court for Army Court Martials that took place at Portsmouth and the chamber is still fitted for them. There are a good many of the old guns on board but a great number have been removed and placed in various museums.

We were shown Nelson's cabin and Captain Hardy's cabin: they were both roomy places but very low. In fact I knocked my head as I walked about in them. There is a brass plate to show the spot where Nelson fell and another to show the place in the cock pit where he died. This spot was covered with laurel wreaths and I suppose they are kept there all the time. The cock pit used to be below the water-line and must have been an awful place when the ship was at sea. In fact I should think all the ship was very uncomfortable as all the decks are low: and they had to keep 1000 men on board. Of course you could hear every man walking above and with 1000 men the noise must have been awful. There were besides two sails shown, one with 90 holes in from round shot and another with 60: in a deckhouse too there were various prints of Nelson and a picture of his death, besides plans of the battles of the Nile, Copenhagen and Trafalgar. In this house were hanging flags showing the signal 'England expects', some of them using the original flags. Besides these we were shown the apparatus for steering the ship, for pumping and for hauling up the anchor: and we had explained the methods of firing the guns.

There were some pieces of the original furniture of the ship and of Nelson's cabin: but most had been removed and distributed to various relatives and institutions. However we spent an interesting half-hour: then we caught our tram and got back to our billet about 8.15.

This week starts the final leave for our battalions. I have asked for mine at the end of this course and this will be the last leave I have before going to the front. I do not know if I shall get it but it will come later if I cannot get it now: and I shall have to be busy because I want to buy a good many things in Bristol. However I will let you know if I get it. The letters you sent me came from Heybridge Hall: you will be interested to hear that Capt & Mrs Fitch have a son now, a baby a month old and Capt Fitch is still in England ...

Candahar Barracks
[Postmarked 2nd May 1916]

Dear Mother
I arrived quite safe last night but was unable to see the Adjutant as he was out: but I shall go and have a chat with him tonight. I have not had a hard time today and am feeling alright: and I do not think there is likely to be much work this week. The Royal Inspection is to come off on Friday next so that I am in time for that.

Col Peyton and the Brigadier have both just left. We have a new Colonel but the new Brigadier has not arrived. It is not known what time we go out but it will probably be next week. There are still however many things to do.

Love to all at home and I trust Walt is better: say goodbye to Harold for me and love especially to father and you.

Candahar Barracks
[Probably 14th May 1916]

Dear Mother
I have got through this week without very much trouble and am feeling a great deal stronger; however last night I had a bad headache but it went after a good night's rest: I am feeling considerably better than I did when I was here before I came home: and as it does not seem that we are going out for a fortnight or so I hope to be quite fit by that time. Where we are going I do not know: the opinion at present seems to be that we shall not go to France but somewhere in the East. In fact it is said that the Brigadier stated we should move shortly and go to the East coast. That means of course that there is fear of an invasion: and I have heard that the War Office are considerably alarmed about it ...

As I told you Colonel Peyton has left us: he is going to be Commandant of the Divisional Base when we get abroad: and so he is not leaving us entirely and we shall see him every time we go on leave or come home for any other reason. The Brigadier, Sir John Barnsley has left us too: but I do not know what he is going to do: I am not sure that he will not go home. Our new Brigadier is an Artillery man, and Stuart is his name. He is a full Brigadier General and so senior to Sir John Barnsley. He is besides a much younger man and he has seen a lot of service in France I believe. Our new Colonel is named Dorman: he comes from the 2nd Worcesters: and he has been in France a lot as well. He too is a younger man ...

The chief event of the week has been the Royal inspection but I have seen no pictures of it and I do not think there were any in any of the illustrated papers. It took place on Friday and we spent Wednesday and Thursday in preparing for it. Wednesday we practised by battalions what we were to do: and on Thursday the Brigade paraded: we saw our new Brigadier for the first time that day and then we marched past and did all we were to do on Friday. On Friday we paraded at about 8.15 and marched off about 9 o'clock. We went across country for about 5 miles and then we arrived at the ground: Bulford Fields[4] was the name of the place. It was a very good ground for it: the ground was level and the grass was short and it was on the side of a slope, with one or two rises and falls so that the spectators could see the troops coming up and down the slopes past the saluting point: and they must have had a very fine sight to see the Division coming over the rises as they were able to get some idea all the time of the numbers on parade. The saluting point, where the King[5] stood to take the salute was just in front of a small wood and there were two enclosures for spectators on either side. We arrived in time to have a rest of about quarter of an hour: then we arose and fixed bayonets, took up our positions and waited for about ten minutes for His Majesty. The King appeared about 11.40 from the left, riding with eight or ten officers with him. On the King's right was Lord French, and with him were Lord Annaly, Commander Sir Somebody Cust, a naval man, Lieutenant General Sclater commanding the Southern Command to which we belong and Lord Salisbury. Behind the King rode an orderly carrying the Royal Standard on a lance and directly the King appeared, a large Royal Standard was hoisted at the Saluting Point. We first gave the Royal Salute: the Division presenting arms, the officers saluting and the band playing 'God Save the King'. The King then rode along the line. Then we marched off to take up positions for the march past. The Divisional Cavalry and cyclists went first and then the Artillery, followed by the Engineers. The Infantry came next, the 182nd Brigade first, that is the Warwicks, then the 183rd Brigade, ourselves, then the 184th Brigade:

then came the R.A.M.C. and the A.S.C. We went by in half companies. I was on the right of the line and had a good view of all who were there: and saw the King very well. After that we marched on and formed up close to a road and took up a line along it and waited for the King to come down. When he came down we all cheered him and the day was done. Again I had a good view as I was out in front. I thought the King was not looking nearly as well as he used to: he seemed much older and much less strong. When he rode down the line he was talking about the disadvantages of yeomanry as he passed us: and I heard one of the Generals behind remark that 'there was a great variety among the faces': whether he meant of the officers or the men I do not know ...

Tomorrow we are going out for a Divisional Scheme and return on Wednesday: we shall be billeted one night and bivouac another: we are going towards Andover about fifteen miles tomorrow but more details I cannot give you as we have not had orders issued yet. Thursday we have to ourselves but Friday we go out at 5pm and return 9 o'clock next morning. So you can see we are not moving this week and I should not think until at least the middle of next week. I shall be very glad to get away from here as this is one of the dullest places you can imagine and

Officers of the 2/7th Battalion, The Worcestershire Regiment outside the officers' mess at Candahar Barracks, Tidworth, prior to embarkation for France in May 1916.
It is difficult to identify SCB.

the continuous bare downs get very monotonous. Anywhere almost will be better than this: I asked Mrs Hopewell, wife of one of our officers if she would ever visit Tidworth again, and she replied firmly 'Never'. So you see I am not alone. As we are likely to be here a bit longer, I shall want some more clothes: will you please send me another pair of pyjamas and another shirt: I have bought another pair of pants of the same kind in Tidworth so that they are alright. My new boots are very comfortable: and thank you very much for the two pairs of socks. I have not been to Church today yet but intend to go this evening ...

I very much enjoyed the five days I had at home and wish they had been longer but I suppose I must do my bit of fighting like everybody else. At any rate I am looking for a good holiday at the end of the War. Best wishes once again and especial love to you all at home ...


Candahar Barracks
[Postmarked 21st May 1916]

Dear Mother

We have had a week partly strenuous and partly slack but the chief event is that we have now definite information of when we leave here. We shall be here for another week and then we leave to go to Southampton and so across to France. The billeting officers are going next Wednesday to arrange for our accommodation and reception: the Divisional staff go next Saturday and the Division begins to embark next Sunday. Of course it will take several days to get it all across, I should think a week at least but Tuesday or Wednesday week we shall go, I should think. This has not been officially published yet but the General of the Division told our officers at a meeting which he held of Commanding Companies: so of course it is authentic. Meanwhile we are getting ready, packing up documents to send back to the Depot and returning stores to the ordnance and getting all the rest ready for despatch abroad. We ought to have fuller information soon; but I am afraid there is no chance of me coming down to say goodbye to you all. I am afraid I shall have to say goodbye by post. As it happened there was weekend leave to be had this week but I did not know about it in time to secure a place as the numbers are very limited: and this was given before the news was out. However Division must have known and it seems rather unfair to give leave and restrict the numbers so very much: no leave ought to have been given at all.

I shall not be sorry to leave Tidworth as I find it a most depressing place:

the air is very dull and dense and makes me very sleepy. I shall be glad to get into a more invigorating atmosphere where I shall feel keener and more energetic. I suppose when we get there it will be a week or two before we are sent into the trenches though of course this depends a lot on the situation at the front. I believe quite a number of troops are being sent to France just now: the 60th Division has been in France a fortnight and we are the 61st. Then besides you have seen how the Australians have been landed in France: and I think it is fairly obvious quite a large number of troops have arrived and are arriving ...

I told you in my last letter that we were to go on a three days Divisional Scheme; it took place on Monday, Tuesday and Wednesday and I came through it quite well. Of course we were carrying on just as if on active service and I had to fill my pack with all it would contain in France and it was a pretty heavy weight. I had of course besides revolver, glasses and haversack and water bottle: as we had a cart to carry our food, we had no need to carry water or food ourselves: nor did the men as we had with us our travelling kitchens. The only other thing I did not carry was revolver ammunition. Well on Monday we marched out and only marched: there was no scheme of operations at all. We started off quite early: we fell in at 7.45 and the battalion formed up and we set off about 8.15. We officers were allowed to take 20 lbs of baggage with us to be carried on a cart. I took my sleeping bag and valise, a pair of slippers and a pair of pyjamas for my 20 lbs. We marched on with regular halts at ten minutes to the hour until about 1 o'clock. We passed through Andover and got about three miles out before we had dinner. We had an hour for dinner and then marched on again until about 3.30 when the brigade formed up in a field behind a farmhouse where we were informed we had to bivouac. As it was very cold and looked rainy this seemed very unpleasant but we set to work to provide shelter as a wind was sweeping up the field; we got hurdles and wattles from the farm and set about placing our waterproof sheets on them to give some slight defence. We had tea but then the rumour came round that there was a change of billets: and presently the C.O. came and told us C Company was to go into billets and we were to toss with another for the chance. We did and won; so we collected our men and marched off into the village at which we had arrived, called St Mary Bourne. One part of a company was put into a farmyard barn with plenty of straw; in the village, the large part into some maltings into two upper rooms where I suppose they had let the malt lie.

The floors were covered with straw and the men slept on it. I got into a cottage just across the road and was given a bed, supper and breakfast for which I had to pay myself. It was however worth it and I slept splendidly between sheets. We had to be up about 7 o'clock next morning so that there was no hurry but it was raining very hard and I felt very glad at having been undercover and I thought of the company which had had to remain out in the open. We started off to march at 9.15 and went on without a halt for an hour and a half. Of course before [we] went we had to clear up our billets and put everything tidy. This day we put out an advanced guard and I was sent right up to the front to lead the Brigade and was given a map to direct the march. It was not hard work but it was interesting as I had to keep an eye on the map and at the same time watch the compass to make sure of keeping right. However I made no mistake and got through that part alright. It was raining for the first hour's march but then it cleared up and we put away our coats. We then went through Andover again but came out on to a different road: we were then sent on to a bye-road to guard the flank of the Brigade as it marched on the main road but were recalled and had to take a side turning back into the main road just in time to see the head of the Brigade go by. So we had to wait while all the Brigade passed and the Transport and then fall in at the rear. It was now about 1 o'clock but we marched for another hour and a half into a village named Wherwell. This part of the march was

Using a periscope
to see the enemy
across No Man's
Land, Tidworth
1916

very trying and the men fell out in good numbers, not our men I am glad to say but chiefly the Gloucesters though it was a difficult job to get our own men along.

We were sent off into a park at Wherwell[6] and there we had dinner but we had some heavy showers of rain which made things unpleasant. But we were sent into billets again, the men had barns and I got another cottage quite close. Wherwell is one of the prettiest villages I have ever seen. There are two streams running through the village, five clear streams running very rapidly: they were waters of the Test and I believe formed one of the finest trout streams in England. The cottages were almost all thatched and there were plenty of trees about and of course, there were flowers everywhere. I had tea in a hotel and had supper in my billet but had to wait up for orders; all the men and everybody had to be in by 7 o'clock in case of an alarm. My men were in a granary by a mill and they spent the evening mostly in going down to the stream and watching the trout, some magnificent fish could be seen just under the bridge, fish more than a foot long and all spotted. I did not get to bed till 11 o'clock and did not sleep well as there were numbers of people passing under the window. But I was aroused by my servant at about 3.20 to tell me we were off in a few minutes and then I heard a company move up. I was dressed in less than ten minutes, pack on and everything just in time to meet the company as it arrived. I fell down stairs but was not hurt and in a few minutes the march started. It was a horrid march; there was a considerable frost and the mist was rising over the river; but the weather was fine. The road was bad and we had constant halts owing to breakdowns to the transport in front but we did not get a halt where we could take off our packs for a long time. We halted at 6 o'clock for breakfast and were given an hour which was extended by another half an hour as it was impossible for the field-kitchens to get breakfast in less. I had a fine breakfast, bacon and eggs with plenty of tea and biscuit instead of bread. I liked the biscuit quite well: this was the biscuit you hear of in 'Bully Beef & Biscuit'. It seems to be made of whole-meal and is shaped like a dog biscuit: so the men won't eat them because of the shape.

We went on after breakfast for a time and halted in a park, Amport Park[7] while the troops were being deployed for an attack. We were in reserve and never came into the attack at all: and operations ceased at 11.8. We then had to march back another 4 or 5 miles to Barracks, the men were awfully tired but we got them along somehow and for the whole day not a man dropped out from our Company. I did the last stretch with the Padre with whom I have made friends, the English Chaplain that is, 'Padre' we call him: and talked about Oxford: it did me a lot of good and I came in feeling quite fresh and not very tired. So you may feel pretty sure I shall be able to stick it in France.

Now, Mother, I will try to write you a few lines before we go out: I am pretty sure to be able to manage that alright, I have no doubt. So please don't worry and when I am abroad I will send, as often as I can, home. Thank you for letter and parcel: I daresay I shall send another parcel of washing this week as I want to go out in clean clothes. Please thank Aunt very much for her letter but I am writing her one in reply. I had a very nice letter too from Uncle Harry and one from Brentwood: letters were brought out to us and both these relaxed me while we were on the 'trek'.

The time is drawing near when we shall be facing the Hun in the trenches but please do not worry about me: I shall be doing what many men have been doing for a year or more and I trust I shall be able to do it as well as they. After all now the best place for an Englishman is out there, at any rate for those Englishmen who are not useful at home: and you must feel glad we are all doing our share. Then the chances of being killed are not very great, one in ten at the highest: for instance our first line battalion has had only two officers killed in a year. I trust I shall be given the strength to endure it all cheerfully and set a good example of patience and fortitude. I entreat you who stay at home to be patient and cheerful too in the time of waiting and trust me to have good fortune and more than that to pray that I do my duty without complaining or shirking. Well I must close as it is getting late: I have been to the village church tonight, not the garrison church and have had a very pleasant service: the Adjutant and Mrs Simpson were there too ...


Candahar Barracks
[Postmarked 23rd May 1916]

Dear Mother

I arrived last night quite safely without any trouble but I walked the last part of the journey from Ludgershall[8] to Tidworth which took me about three quarters of an hour. It was very annoying to be in so early: I should have liked to have spent more of the day with you but I could not. Today I have been just packing up and putting everything ready for tomorrow. We shall be going soon after mid-day but I cannot say what further arrangements will be made after that. I have sent off tonight my kit-bag containing everything I am not taking with me: it includes two blankets which have been issued to me: keep them carefully please as I may want them sooner or later.

Now, mother, please be cheerful while I am away because after all it is only right that I should go: and many and many others have gone to do more than I: it is the right place for all Englishmen now and we are only taking a small part in a great work. If God wills, I shall come back to you safe and sound: if I do not, why there is nothing hard in dying for a great cause: after all it is the cause that matters and not the life of this individual or that. I trust God will give me courage, patience and endurance in danger and hardship and I hope only to do my duty as an English gentleman: and these things are greater and worthier than long life or safety. So please be patient until I return again.

I will try to write as regularly as possible but though my letters will not be censored you must not expect me to tell you anything that will show where I am or details of what we are doing.

So goodbye to you all ...

Love to Miss Green and remember me to Mr and Mrs Guy and Ray; love to every one of you, to Aunt, Harold and Walter. I trust Walter is not feeling too tired after his first day of business again. Love to each one of you and best wishes for everyone. I was very glad to see you all before going and know that you are all well: please do not worry about me: and love once again, especial love to father and yourself.


[23rd May 1916]
Dear Mother

I forgot these things when sending the rest home. Please thank Walt for his watch and please look after the rest.
We take train at 3 o'clock today.

Our address now will be:
Lieut. Booker
2/7th Worcesters
B.E.F.
France

Love to everyone ...

The 926 men and 35 officers of the battalion left Southampton on ss *Caesarea* at 6pm on 23rd May but by the next morning they were back in Southampton dock. A warning of submarines had led to a return to safety. They eventually arrived in Le Havre on 25th May and went to a rest camp. The movements of the battalion during its time in France can be followed in detail from the entries in the official War Diary kept by Col Dorman, Major Grainger and Major Green.

It had been decided that the 61st Division should hold a quiet section of the front in Flanders and not join the preparations for the Battle of the Somme. They were sent to the front near Neuve Chapelle and Laventie, about 15 miles east of Bethune and 25 miles south of the Belgian border. This was low lying country, criss-crossed by streams and drainage ditches and often flooded in winter. The reason for the decision was that the 61st had some weaknesses. As Stanley's letters indicate, they had been issued with rifles and Lewis guns only a short time before embarkation, they had no time to train properly with them and a major purge of senior officers had taken place just before leaving England. The whole Division was under strength.

On 25th May the battalion left Le Havre in trains for Berguette and the following day they marched 10 miles to Robecq where the front line was 23 miles to the east. The next few days were taken up with church parades, lectures, inspections and route marches. Towards the end of the week the battalion marched to Vieille Chapelle where they were billeted and on Thursday 1st June they moved into the trenches at Richebourg-Saint-Vaast. Four days later they were relieved and this became the pattern for the months ahead. In all the time he was in France Stanley was in the front trenches on eleven separate occasions for a total of 57 days and at rest camps for 79 days. The battalion War Diary lists the tasks undertaken in the trenches – repairing parapets and wire, replying to the enemy, sending across artillery bombardment, making raids and collecting the wounded and the dead. The

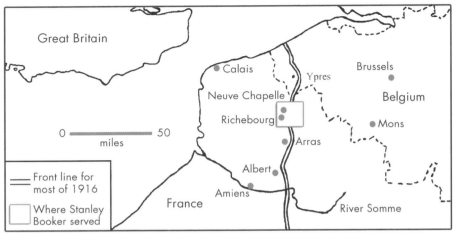

Part of the Western Front 1916

activities undertaken during the rest periods were fairly predictable – bathing, cleaning kit, inspections, aeroplane signalling and on a lighter note, horse shows, relay races and a football match against the 2/6th Gloucesters which was a draw 1-1.

Although this section of the front was relatively quiet the objective was to cause the enemy enough trouble to discourage him from sending reinforcements south to the Somme. The Diary regularly records: 'Heavy bombardment 10.0pm to 10.30pm. Considerable damage to enemy's parapet and wire …1 company and 2 machine guns entered German trenches at N 19 A 7.6; did considerable damage with bombs to Germans in trenches and dugouts … 4 officers wounded, other ranks killed 2, wounded 31.' Eventually it was decided to launch a major assault on 19th July. This became known as the Fromelles attack and it was a disaster. The 61st Division was sent into attack with the 5th Australian near Neuve Chapelle and Festubert. There was confusion over the plan, none of the 61st reached German lines, there were over 7000 casualties and thereafter the 61st was perhaps unfairly given the nickname 'The Sixty Worst'. The 2/7th Worcesters played no part in the attack but were moved up afterwards to take over from the Gloucesters who suffered very heavy casualties in the Fauquissart section. In the words of the Worcestershire Regiment historian, 'The attack had been a disastrous failure.

The two brave Gloucestershire battalions had suffered terribly, the trenches were shattered and the ground in front was littered with dead and wounded.'

It was at this point that Stanley was awarded the Military Cross. A major task after the attack was to search for and bring in the dead and wounded. The search began on 20th July at night but when day dawned on 21st July there were still wounded men lying unclaimed in No Man's Land. Despite the enemy's sharp and deadly fire, Stanley and two others were determined to continue the search. They all brought in more wounded men and Stanley's citation reads: 'For conspicuous gallantry. Assisted by another officer and two men he brought in 14 wounded men from No Mans Land under heavy fire. Next day, with two men, he brought in a wounded officer from within 30 yards of the enemy's parapet.' Stanley was told about the award during the last week of July. He described the rescue in a letter home but the longest account, including his attempt to search for Langford his old team mate from the school 1st XV of 1910, is in a letter to his former Headmaster Dr Norwood. (This and a previous letter describing life in the trenches are reproduced by kind permission of the Keeper of The Special Collections and Archives, the University of Sheffield).

By late September the nights were becoming long although it was still warm and the trees retained their leaves. The plan was that the 61st Division should be relieved by the 56th Division at the end of October and make their way south to prepare to fight in the Battle of the Somme. Stanley did not participate. He was killed on 10th October 1916.


2/7th Worcesters
BEF
France
[Probably late May 1916]

Dear Mother

I am now quartered in a comfortable little village in France quite peacefully within twelve miles of the firing line: we can hear the guns very distinctly at times. However from the appearance of this village you would hardly think there was a war on this half of the globe at any rate. The men as usual are billeted in barns and so on in the farm houses, while the officers are in houses close by. I am quite comfortable and have a bed to sleep on.

We have not been here long: and had a 21 hours railway journey to get here: and we crossed half France very nearly to get in. Then we marched 8 miles or so and arrived here quite late: then we had to allot quarters and I was dead tired when I got to bed. But I was roused early by the sound of geese as my room looks out on the farm yard and is on the bottom floor. These wretched birds began to scream as early as it got light and every time they did it they woke me up. I did not mind the guns but these wretched geese were too much for me.

Tuesday

I have not been able to write continuously as you see because I have had quite a lot to do without having anything very big on hand. We are having very good weather and the country is at its best I suppose now: everything is very green and the landscape is very tidy: every foot of ground almost is used for agriculture. There are very few hedges and the land is very flat where we are: but there are quite a number of trees which are usually in clumps or in rows not as in England dotted about everywhere.

Everywhere we have been we have seen women and practically only women working in the fields. There are a very few men about who are not in uniform and they are chiefly old. Another thing I have noticed is the piles of stores of all sorts about everywhere and the business of the ports and railways. The railways here however are not nearly as neat and tidy as in England and they do not seem nearly as well managed. But there is not so very much difference in other things: the houses in the villages seem older and less sanitary and generally bedrooms and living rooms are on the same floor. However these are the houses of the peasantry and I have not seen many of the wealthier classes about here. I like the French peasantry very much: here at any rate they are quite friendly and they seem a quiet, peaceful and simple folk.

I find the French I learnt at school quite useful and I can make myself understood in the simpler sentences. I can read a French newspaper without difficulty as well. My letters are not censored here: but I daresay they are at the Base. I have to censor my own men's letters and they have given me a lot to do: so that I have hardly time to write myself.

Now I must close if I am to catch the post tonight. However I must thank you for your two letters both of which I have had. Especial love to father and yourself and Aunt; best wishes for you all and please do not worry about me as I am well and happy.

BEF
France
[Postmarked 6th June 1916]

Dear Mother

There is no news since I wrote you the last letter really except that I may not be able to write again for a few days: so please do not be worried if you do not hear from me for a time. I warned you I should not be able to write regularly and I have only been able to write my last two letters because we have not done much and we are now going to be busy.[1] But I will not keep you without news longer than I can help it.

My chief reason for writing is that I want to ask you to send me a newspaper or two so that I can see what happened in this naval battle.[2] I should like especially if you could send me this week's copy of 'Land and Water' which will come out next Friday. It costs sixpence and it will give a review of all the events of the War for the week and I should like especially to see this number. Please send me out a parcel of food sometimes, just luxuries which are not included in Army rations. We get plenty to eat but it does not include anything but necessaries. I will send you a cheque over pretty soon so that if I want anything you can get it from that money. I would like something that can be shared out if you do send anything. However you need not send very often: and please use everything of mine which is of use to you. If I am out here for the winter some of the clothes I have left behind will be useful so please keep them all locked up.

I think I have no more news except that this naval battle has aroused much interest here and we want to know all about it. I think I had better close now but I can tell you we are near a very famous village.[3] However if you would just look out for those things for me I would be very glad ...

Tuesday

P.S. I went to church parade on Sunday and to the Holy Communion in a shed here afterwards, quite a short service. SCB

P.P.S. By the way, what you have heard about the crossing is quite true. We were in the first boat that night, got quite close to Havre and then had to turn around and race back again pursued by a submarine. Besides that the destroyer which was our escort collided with us: it tried to cross our bows but had not room so had to swing round and then its stern knocked against our bows and made a pretty big dent but nothing serious. It is said our destroyer saw the submarine and tried to ram it by running across our bows. At any rate we had a narrow escape. We have not been able to talk about [it] till now: so that is why I did not tell you. Next day we spent in Southampton and crossed safely that night.

B.E.F.
France
[Dated July 12th 1916]

Dear Mother

I hope now to get you off a longer and more detailed letter than I was able to yesterday. As I told you we have done a week in the trenches and had a pretty warm time. I cannot give you full details of everything that happened but the battalion made a raid such as you often see mentioned in the papers[4]: it was not so completely successful as we would like; it no doubt tickled the Hun up considerably and it gave him more than he gave us. It cost us some officers but none were killed and all are now getting on nicely we understand. They are back in England by this time: we did not have more than two men killed but several were wounded most of them only slightly. I was not in it as only a part of the battalion took part and that did not include my Company. I do not think I can tell you more about it: in fact I know very little of it but all who went in agree in praising the conduct of Captain Tomkinson who after being wounded went on directing operations and threw bomb after bomb at the Germans and did not mention his wound until all were in our trenches again. Every night however we had an evening 'strafe': it started exactly the same time every night and lasted about half an hour each night. We knew exactly where the German shells would fall and of course we were able to prepare for them: they would put shells each time over the same bit of trench and rarely did one come anywhere else. Besides shells they always sent off a trench mortar or two: these are horrid things: they make a terrific light and crash but their one virtue is that you can see them coming as they leave a trail of sparks behind them. After about half an hour all would cease and we would settle down for the night and generally nothing much more would happen. Of course the Germans did not have it all their own way: in fact they got generally more than we did as our artillery has now plenty of shells and are quite good. Besides these little affairs at night we had one or two day bombardments by aerial torpedoes. These are fired from some sort of gun I believe because you can hear a pop on discharge and then you hear a whizz and down they come: they have a pointed head, a stick and a tail with fins which acts as a propeller. You can distinguish the report on discharge and can see them coming besides hear them. So if you keep a sharp look out you can always get under shelter. The first day we had between twenty and thirty of them over but none was hit. Two fell about 15yds from me as I was talking to another officer but neither of us was touched except by falling earth. It was rather amusing the first day to watch everyone run round corners every time one was heard: but next day when we had only half a dozen my corporal was hit in the head: he died the same night poor fellow. He was my best Corporal and a splendid fellow altogether: no one could have been a greater help to me and I will miss him dreadfully. He was all a soldier ought to be, brave, resourceful, clever and cheerful and we shall not do so well without him. He was buried the day we came out of the trenches and the Captain let me go early to attend the funeral with three men. We had a cart to take us and he is buried in a cemetery which holds more than 1100 English dead besides French, Hindus and Germans. I learnt a lot during the stay and feel that I shall be quite up to the ordinary routine of trench warfare in future. There was a lot going on each side of us: artillery bombardments and raids took place more than once: and we could see the 'strafe' quite clearly but in our Company front we did not have a shell except the last night, though as I have told you they came close to us on my right every night.

You will be glad to hear I stood it better than I expected. I did not go to bed at all except during day time: I was up and about all the time it was dark and busy. I had plenty to think about all the time and during the night I never got more than quarter of an hour's rest. But the men stood it splendidly and behaved grandly and now they will be getting quite seasoned troops. They were all very cheerful and only too glad to get a shot at the Germans. One man of mine shot two Germans in broad daylight and was awfully pleased about it. On the night of our raid when there were plenty of bullets flying about, I could not keep them down below the parapets: I had to drag them down and tell them it was not a show for them to watch.

One thing you quickly learn out here is that our airmen are really all over the Germans. I have not seen a German aeroplane yet though I believe some have been about. At any rate they always go so high as to be mere specks while ours are quite low sometimes: it was very interesting to watch one who could not have been more than 3000 ft up, dodge the German shrapnel and each time he flew out of a ring of shells he gave them a salute from his machine gun. He was very clever indeed in the way he dodged them and got away quite unhurt. He did not hurry away either but finished his work first.[5]

We are still within reach of shell fire in a little town where every house shows marks of splinters. But only one has come here yet but last week it was shelled frequently. The Germans are good at shelling roads: one road we went down had been searched most methodically on each side, there was a shell hole every ten yards, none of them very recent. However another road I came along had in one spot a mass of shell holes all quite fresh and on each side too. It really had been shelled but I think no one was caught there. It is wonderful how ineffective shelling generally is. We have had shells each night but hardly a man has been hit though we had enough to wipe out a battalion easily. It was a great sight to watch them shelling a ruined church one night: every shell pitched in it and sent up a huge cloud of dust but it did us no damage at all.

I am glad to be able to tell you I have come out quite safe though I had a bit of everything to do. Of course I was very tired at the end of it and very sleepy but I am making up for it now. We shall go in again soon but we are not anywhere near the big push at present[6] though I expect that will extend and I have no doubt before it ends we shall have our share to do. Please do not send me any more newspapers now as we get them quite regularly and I see them all before yours reach me: the arrangement we made is in working order but thank you very much all the same for them. I received your first parcel in the trenches where it was very welcome and soon disappeared. The dates arrived the day we came out and they too have gone: so you see your gifts could not have come at a better time. The prunes and fruit were exactly what we wanted in the trenches and filled a gap splendidly. I thank you very much indeed for them.

I am going to write to Doctor Norwood soon if I can manage it and also to Oxford to let them know how I am getting on. I shall have to send to Dunscombe's besides for spectacles and I think I shall ask them to send them with the bill to you, and please meet the expense from the cheque. Tell me at once won't you, directly that £5 is getting low and I will send more. We get more money out here than at home and less chance to spend it so that I can well spare money for all that sort of thing and I do not want you to pay for my things. I have met no friends out here other than I had at Tidworth but I daresay I shall before long. I do not know how close we are to Webb[7], or anyone else but you have some surprising meetings out here sometimes.

Well I think I must close now as it is getting near dinner time: but please do not worry about me as I am quite alright …

B.E.F.
France
[Probably mid July 1916]

Dear Dr Norwood,
It is very nearly two months since we left England and our adventures
began at once. We left Southampton for Havre one evening and nearly
reached the other side when we were turned back because of submarines.
We seemed to have had the closest shave of the whole squadron: and in
fact we collided with our escorting destroyer which attempted to cross
our bows. Why she should have tried such a risky thing I do not know but
it is said a submarine was sighted just on our right and she tried to ram
it. However the result was a collision but no damage was done as the
destroyer swung outwards and her stern caught us in the bows. We were
all shaken up but soon retired again and in the morning found ourselves
in Southampton again instead of Havre. We crossed however without
adventure the next night: and after a night in camp came up to the front
and within a week were within range of shell fire and in the trenches
shortly afterwards: and since then we have been carrying on. So far I
have been quite unharmed either by the enemy or the fatigues out here
but I have had some narrow escapes all the same.

We have just completed a turn in the trenches and had rather a lively
time though we are nowhere near the Somme. In the middle of the tour
the Germans opposite were relieved apparently and it was interesting to
notice the differences between the two sets of troops. The first were
evidently an inferior regiment because we could do what we liked with
them and we made them very jumpy. We raided them one night and the
next they were evidently very nervous because they kept sending up lights
and were continually firing and they brought up a searchlight to make
quite sure we were not coming over again. The next lot were much more
enterprising. They started to give us aerial torpedoes of a small pattern,
we could not put a tin on a parapet without having a shot sent at it and
they started patrolling at night and came up close to our line. These
torpedoes are horrid things: they have a trail to guide them but
fortunately you can distinguish the sound of discharge and watch them
coming over. We had nearly 30 over in an hour one night but no one was
hit: but next day we had six and one man was killed. We hear they are
still sending them over on to the battalion which relieved us: and if we go
in again at the same place we will try to knock them out.

It is curious how methodical the Boche is: every night we used to have a 'strafe': it started punctually at 10.00 o'clock, continued for half an hour and stopped. They always had too certain spots to fire at and we always knew where they would shell. However it was unpleasant all the same: several shells used to burst just short of the line I had in my charge but I had no man hit. After that everything used to finish unless we started shelling and then we might have a few more. Since we came out of line I think even this has been stopped and everything is quiet except of course when we get up a show.

We are at a spot where there was terrific fighting last year and I have seen some wonderful sights. There is a road I know leading to the enemy line where there is a shell hole every ten yards: I counted the paces from one to another and they occurred regularly. The town we are in is the same too: nearly every house has been shelled and although some are still fit for habitation most are knocked out. Civilians are still living here in fairly large numbers though most of the inhabitants are gone and these are largely refugees. The church is entirely burned: one wall of the tower is still standing: the roof is lifted off entirely and every window is gone. I have been too in a village which is known all over England, it is about 300 yards behind the firing line. Every house is in ruins; some are only a couple of walls: there is no roof in the whole place and the communications wind in and out under house walls and through gardens. There is a church there but I could not recognise it and there is a chateau too. The trenches run through the gardens but there are still roses to be gathered there if you take the trouble to crawl and not show yourself: and each dug out had a few hanging there. There are many other interesting things I have seen that I know you would like to hear but I am afraid I must postpone that until it is all over: we have had a very interesting bit of line indeed to hold.

I must close now as time is running short; I do not get much time for letters and when I begin a letter it may be a week before I can close it as we are having a very busy time indeed. But please remember me to Mrs Norwood who I trust is in the best of health and the Miss Norwood. I presume school will be breaking up shortly and you will be having a change though perhaps not a holiday. However I wish you the best of good times and a happy interlude and

I remain, Sir

Yours very sincerely

Stanley Booker

BEF
France
[Dated 27th July 1916]

Dear Mother

As we are now out of the trenches again[8] I am able to write you a letter to show you I am quite well. But we have had a very busy time during the last fortnight and had to take part in an attack which has been described in the papers.[9] When I wrote my last letter we were very busy with fatigue parties all day long getting up stores and supplies and we were out at all hours. Some of the parties had a very rough time as they got shelled as they were carrying stuff up and we had some casualties but none serious. However a few men of other battalions were killed. The attack came off a week ago: we were not in it thank God, for some of the battalions were very badly hit: and the two of our Brigade had it worst of all. I daresay you will have heard of it by now in Bristol for the two Bristol battalions suffered heavily especially in officers. Capt Rudman and Jack Langford are both missing, they must both be lying dead somewhere in 'No Man's Land' between the two lines. We came into the trenches that night and I was told about Langford and I went out after dark to try and find him but though I searched all night I could not find him. A lance-corporal of my platoon whom I took out with me was killed when crawling along a yard behind me. A machine opened on us and he was hit through the head and killed at once while it all passed over me. But you may be sure it gave me a nasty shock and I lay low for a while until I thought it safe to go on. We brought in quite a lot that night but there were numbers of bodies we could not get in at all. Next day when it was light an officer could be seen not far from the German lines trying to attract attention by waving a handkerchief, shouting and blowing a whistle. We could not get him in by day: so we had to wait until night and meanwhile a German saw him and brought an officer to see him. So we were afraid they would try to get him first: but a party went out and brought him back alright without meeting any Germans. I was hoping it would turn out to be Langford but it was not so. It was an officer attached to them named Metcalfe. He was quite clear-headed and conscious and as brave as you can find them. He had mistaken the German lines for ours and when the party reached him he threatened them with a revolver but they managed to persuade him they were friends and he was soon in. He stated quite distinctly Langford was dead and as I have since heard he was put for shelter into the same hole as Langford. I am afraid there is no hope that Langford is even a prisoner.

We too have lost two fine officers during this tour. Capt Butcher and Lt Johnson. Both were hit outside the trenches in our wire: they apparently were seen by some German who was outside as well: and as it was not dark but only dusk when they went out the distance he was in front of their lines would make all the difference. They were hit on following nights and are a great loss to us. Butcher I should think had earned more respect than any other officer in the battalion for the fine chap he was. Straight, clean, brave and kindly he was what every Englishman wishes to be and no one was more loved or respected than he. So was Johnson too: but he had not been with us so long. Butcher had been with the battalion from the beginning and his sister had married another of our officers, Capt Hopewell who was wounded some time back. They were inseparable and it will be a terrible blow for him and his wife.

This battalion has suffered and we are beginning to be veterans already: we know what it is to lose our best and yet it does not unnerve us. War is a horrible thing out here: it is so brutal and yet the Germans are quite right: there is something inspiring and noble about it and when I think of those two Bristol battalions who lost so heavily especially in officers when all their leaders were killed, yet falling in and carrying on it is impossible not to see there is something grand about it. Duty surpasses everything and overcomes sorrow and fear and goes on as usual in the most appalling circumstances. When we arrived in the trenches that night there was blood and dead men all over the place: the parapet was breached and the communication trenches choked, dugouts were smoking and wounded were lying on the duckboards and the fallen lay in front of us in rows: while everywhere equipment, food, bombs, ammunition lay littered about. The whole place was confusion but we settled down to work at once and by morning the parapet was standing as before and some of the rubbish had been cleared: and in two days the trenches were clear. It was enough to frighten anybody what we saw when we arrived but the men soon settled down and were as cheery as usual. And for myself there seems something great and noble in that sort of thing.

Thank you very much for letters and parcel: they have all been very welcome. The currants were in perfect condition and we had them stewed that night in the trenches. Capt Boucher and the other officers were very pleased with them: so you can feel sure they were appreciated. It was very good of you to think of me: they were such a delightful change and your parcels of that sort give pleasure to others besides me so that you see you are doing a lot when you send that sort of thing: the gooseberries were a bit smashed: I gave them to the servants to sort and they had what there were to eat. I saw one night in the trenches that Dr Norwood had been appointed Headmaster of Marlborough: it was about the only time I picked up a paper the whole time.

B.E.F.
France
[Begun 8th August, finished 16th August]
Dear Mother

We are really out of the trenches this time and are some distance behind the line quite out of the range of shell fire.[10] This is a relief because ever since our last rest we have been within range of the German guns: all through July and the first week of August we were liable to be shelled at any minute: for five weeks we were in that danger and as we were in the middle of batteries it might come off at any moment. Fortunately it did not. However for the present we are within sound of the guns but out of range and you can be sure we are very glad to be able to get a rest.

Now three weeks have passed and I can tell you a little more about the attack this division made. Another division composed of Australians were to join us in making it and together I suppose we were to seize a mile of trench. We had been out of the trenches two days when the authorities began to require large working parties: and after two days more the fun became furious. The men were out all day: all the twenty hours we were supplying men for various duties, carrying stores chiefly but also for building various emplacements. One Saturday afternoon from 2 to 8.30pm. I had a party carry trench mortar shells through nearly a mile of communication trench. That night a gas attack was made for gas had been put in the trenches some time previously but I believe the Hun was prepared for it: at any rate he retaliated on the trenches for about three hours with every possible form of iron, rifle grenades, torpedoes, trench mortars and artillery of all sorts. We were not in the trenches for that: one battalion which was came through it all without a casualty. Meanwhile the enemy must have learnt something was on: because he began to collect artillery. This day he did not seem very strong but next day when we went on with all these preparations he used more batteries and gave us quite a heavy shelling in the morning. Some of our gas cylinders were hit in the trenches and leaked and a good number of men were gassed in that way, one or two fatally. For some reason or other the attack was put off for two days and instead of taking place on a Monday it took place on a Wednesday. We had been in readiness all Saturday night and Sunday all day: but we were allowed to rest on Monday and Tuesday so called but the men had an awful time: they were working on carrying parties all day and all night and had hardly any rest for a week. Nor did the officers have much. But everyone had a good rest Tuesday night because the attack was to take place on Wednesday.

We had a soft morning and afternoon: we did very little beyond seeing everything was ready: the Coy. I am in and another being first reserves and if the trenches had been taken it would have been our job to go in and hold them against counter-attack. The bombardment started at 1 o'clock but really you cannot say it started at any one time because the guns were always on! But still all had orders to join in at 1 o'clock. This went on all the afternoon and just before six the first waves of the attack went over. On the night of the attack they got over with scarcely any loss but as you know our brigade were cut down by machine gunfire: and on the left the other division managed to get in. They were Australians and it is said they went through the first and support lines and even got to the German billets which they set on fire. But in each case they could not be supported and had to fall back.[11] Of course most of those who got through never came back at all and are missing. Most are killed of course but several I dare say are alive as prisoners of war. It would be much more interesting if I could give you the names of which regiment did which but I must not in case of accidents. However we got the order to move at about 6 and were shelled as we left our billets. All of the shells fell beyond us and in my company no one was hurt but two men I think were slightly wounded in the company that went up with us. We got into the communication trenches and picked up bombs and ammunition to carry and take to the men in front of us. We did not use the trenches beyond a certain point as they were always shelled but made our way up ditches. We got into the front line and found the attack had failed and everyone exhausted and shortly afterwards came the order that we were to relieve the battalion that had been in all day.

I have told you how we found the trenches: and our work for the next week was to put up more wire, clear out all the stores of ammunition and bombs, iron rations and everything else, helped by various fatigue parties sent up. Our trenches were bad enough but the Germans' were awful: the wire had almost all disappeared: and their parapets were no more than a lump of earth. When we arrived one of our big howitzers was still shelling the German front line and each shell came with the noise of an express train and burst with a crash and sent up showers of earth. Fighting was still going on, on the right and went on all night. The

Germans claim to have counted 2000 corpses in front of the line as a result of the attack: this is an exaggeration: the whole losses of the division including everyone, killed, wounded and missing in all arms cannot have been much more. They had one or two lucky hits however: they burst one of their shells in an observation post and killed 4 officers and 3 men of the Artillery, one of whom a Major, came from Clifton.

I have told you about our tour in the trenches that time: the last time we were in the line was uneventful though the usual routine went on. I had charge of the Lewis Guns at that time and though it was harder work it was more interesting and I am an independent commander and of more importance than the ordinary platoon commander. The Lewis Gun Officer was in charge of a company. Well when we got out of the line we found we had a new C.O. Col Dorman had left us and Major Grainger had been in charge ever since Col Dorman had been in hospital. We all thought Major Grainger would be made our Colonel when another Major arrived to take over. It meant everyone went down a step and of course many were upset by it. I had to give up the Lewis Guns and go back to the Coy. again. But now Major Grainger has gone back to England on a month's leave and all go back again: and as the Lewis Gun Officer is on a course near Boulogne I get the guns again. And this time I think it will be permanent. With a little luck it will. I have a horse now of my own and have to ride. I have been learning here and am getting on nicely. I have quite a good looking horse and will have to have boots and spurs. And of course in the trenches I shall be independent very largely.

Last time I had one or two narrow escapes as the Germans always fired back at us when we opened fire and they swept our parapets with great accuracy. However neither a man or gun was hit and we had no casualties. We got to work to reply and I think we had some success for the enemy's fire after that was nothing like so hot. One night it was almost incessant but much less the following nights. The mornings were very misty so that you could almost walk over to the German trenches without being seen. Some of our men went over and found a machine gun which had been lying out there a fortnight and ammunition with it. They brought it back and fired with it at once. They also found some dead Germans and brought in everything that could give us information from them. There were besides plenty of our dead – killed in the attack we made. We have been at rest for a week but I have been very busy in a quiet way taking over the Lewis Gun Section and so on, including learning to ride in the afternoons so that I have had not much time for letters. In fact this letter has taken me a week to write. I am afraid Bristol will have lost heavily.

Capt Eyre has died of wounds and Lieut Briggs who came from Stoke Bishop was killed some time previously. I knew them both. I had a talk with Major Langford and I told him all I knew about his brother. He is officially reported 'Believed killed' now and I am afraid we must put him down as dead. So too with Capt Rudman. We have had no more casualties in officers though one or two of our men have been hit. Well I must not go on any more but I wish you would get for me a reliable electric torch light, small enough to carry in the pocket and one or two refills with it: and also a pair of officers puttees. And please also send me two pairs of socks and one or two of my khaki handkerchiefs. Please use the money I sent you and tell me how much is left of it ...

P.S. I have had more parcels from Jessie Stebbing: she is very good to send them and letters with them.

SCB on horseback near Neuve-Chapelle, France in 1916.
He was very proud of learning to ride but looks uncomfortable

BEF
France
[Probably mid August 1916]
Dear Mother

I have been out of the trenches one day now: we were not in for more than four days and we had a fairly quiet time but there were one or two little incidents which were interesting and fairly exciting. On our front line there were a lot of mine craters, about a dozen just in front of our line and two we held. One of them was blown up by the Germans while another Brigade of our division was in and the battalion there had a very bad time. It went up right under the trench and they lost about 40 men in it. It was right in the middle of their front line. But they kept the Germans out and the Germans probably lost quite as heavily as we did. However our line has been built round it now and it is secure. But there is always mining going on on this particular bit of front and one morning right in the middle of No Mans Land a small mine went up. It was the Germans who were trying to blow in one of our galleries under the earth but they did not do much damage. However that night we had to blow up their gallery at about the same place and we made a much better job of it. When these things are blown up they send up a big shoot of flame and then all the earth comes falling down again. There is no noise more than a rumble but the earth shakes for a long way round. Generally after a mine goes up there is a heavy bombardment but there was nothing either time for which we were very thankful.

Another interesting incident was the fact that I had to take out a patrol and try and kill some Germans with a Lewis Gun. We hoped to find them putting up wire in front of their lines so we could fire at them. I went out into these craters I told you about and got within 50 yards or so of the German parapets and though we could hear them working behind the lines and talking we could not see one. I fired my revolver to attract attention in case a German patrol might come out to see what was going on but no one left their trenches. So I fired nearly 100 rounds from the Lewis Gun at their trenches but even that did not bring them out and so I returned. It seems almost impossible to find Germans outside their trenches in this part of the front: they keep pretty close and it is thought they are troops who have been to the Somme and now want a quiet time. However we did not allow them to have it entirely quiet because we gave them plenty of bombs from our Stokes guns and trench mortars. The Stokes guns are very effective and they can fire very rapidly. They are not used so much for killing men as for knocking in parapets and trenches and for cutting the wire. Of course they do this very well if they are pitched on the right place: but with all these weapons, even artillery there is great uncertainty and it is absolutely essential that there should be no fault in the charging of them or in the cartridges used to fire them if one wishes for success. Again if they fit the gun too tightly or too loosely the result is the same: they must be entirely reliable in every way. We have been in a part of the line we were in when we first came out but it has altered very much so that at first I could not find my way about. Trees which in June were quite thick with leaves were now only bare stumps: that is the result of shell fire and other high explosives. The whole place looks more desolate: only the chateau gardens were as beautiful as before but one day as I was just coming to them as I was going out of the trench I was sniped: the bullet fairly whizzed past me. I had two men with me but it was a clear miss. I did not stop to admire the chateau gardens. I did spend an hour one morning looking round the village but I told you of that.

We are again out of reach of shell-fire for a short time in a place where we were some weeks ago. I have not got the same billet but still I am fairly comfortable and have a bed in a room overlooking the street so I can

Soldiers billeted in a typical French farm

amuse myself quite well if I have nothing better to do. We see plenty of supply wagons and motor lorries here: and today a battery of big guns each drawn by a traction engine followed by half a dozen lorries passed through. There is no doubt that on our part of the front we can take liberties with the Germans but I doubt if we were really to attack whether we should get the easy job that it appears at first sight. The Germans lie quiet a good deal but they never let go anything without a fight for it and really are quite good opponents. Where they beat us is that they are more systematic and organised in their defences though we could be as good as they are if we chose. Only the Englishman I suppose is made too casual to trouble to provide for things he thinks unlikely to happen and it seems to me a German attack on this part of the line or indeed any part is a very unlikely matter. I think here he is good enough to be left alone. Still it was a surprise to us the strength he showed when we made that attack last July.

The war seems to be going very well for us at present but you must not expect it to end for some months yet. We are wearing the Germans out and that is all. By and by we may be able to do bigger things but we are not sufficiently superior yet to expect big and sensational results. However, everywhere we possess the initiative and even since the time we came out things have changed. When we first arrived and first held trenches in this part of the line, it was the Germans who gave us a hard time: they started all the little shows that went on, they frequently patrolled No Man's Land but now it is changed. We start the bombardments and we do the patrolling and we cannot find any Germans outside their trenches when we look for them. We have very good trench mortars, the Mediums and Stokes Gun I know chiefly: and the Germans stand in mortal dread of them. We can never let them off without drawing immediate retaliation. We always know when we annoy the Germans because they always fire back. We had no serious casualties this time in the lines I am glad to say. Well I think I must close if this letter is to go today.

P.S. Thanks very much for the parcel and Land and Water. Would like to hear how Walt is getting on and if he had a new job in testing those shells or whether it is the same as before. I am always interested to hear of 'Mr Alfred' and everyone else down there and what is going on. How is the Vicar and Fred Summer? What is Harold doing now? Where is Mr Bolt? What about the Bristol Battalion, Jack Webb, Wilfred, Bingham Hall and all the others I remember at Ashton Gate? I have seen nothing of them out here.

BEF
France
[Dated Sunday 3rd September]

Dear Mother

It is now more than a fortnight since we left our rest billets and I have been very busy: my new job gives me more work to do than before but now I am able to have an easier time as I have got most of the initial work over. As it happens I sent off my last letter the day before we left our rest. We marched out the next day and the day after that went into the trenches. It was not the same place and was a much more unpleasant part of the line, where the enemy had aerial torpedoes and trench mortars. Nothing of great importance happened there though we were only 70 or 80 yards from the Germans: and it was easy to hear them laughing and talking at night. I also saw one or two working one early morning before it was fully light. We have moved again and have just come out from another part of the line. Here it was also very unpleasant because we indulged in little 'strafes' as we call them. Our trench mortars, Stokes guns and artillery would fire daily at various points in the Hun Line and the Hun used invariably to retaliate. He used trench mortars and aerial torpedoes: both of which are very nasty. They drop into the trench and then explode.

Well I had a nasty experience one day. We had just finished one of our 'strafes' when the Hun started again. He began to send over his trench mortar shells (Minenwerfer), we call them 'Minnies'. I was outside a firebag just seeing if some of my men were alright when we heard a pop and knew he was sending over one of these. We looked for it and saw it was going to drop close: so we hurried into shelter. As it happens it fell twenty yards away, about: it dropped into a slimy pool and sent up a great column of liquid mud which covered me as it fell and all who were around. It was horrid, stinking stuff and as I went down the line it was amusing to see the open mouths and wide eyes of all who saw me. Not a man was hurt but it was a lucky escape. However we turned the artillery on to the gun and they kept quiet for some time.

Walter will be interested to know I have met a friend of his out here: a man named Stockley who is in the other battalion of the Worcesters in our Brigade. He spoke to me one morning and said he knew my brother: and I promised to tell Walter when I wrote. This man is a sniper and has an interesting and rather easy job though a bit dangerous unless one is very careful. I am sorry to see that Dr Dawes' son who won the DSO for

Worcestershire Territorials resting *en route* for the front; the stretcher bearers are wearing white armbands

flying over Gallipoli and sinking the Turkish transport is missing. I happened to see that in the Daily Mail one day. Another friend CS Lewis I regret to say has been wounded this last time in the trenches though not very seriously. It will however take him out of his regiment I expect.

My servant has been awarded the Military Medal for services he rendered in bringing in wounded the night of the big Divisional attack. A corporal was given the same decoration for the same deed. Both were from my platoon.

As for myself, I am proud to be able to tell you I have just been granted the Military Cross. The award was published one day last week while we were in the trenches. I am already wearing the ribbon and I am entitled to put MC after my name: and I daresay one day I shall have to go to Buckingham Palace to receive the medal. But we shall see. At any rate though it is published officially out here, it will not be in the Gazette for another three or four weeks I expect.[12] Look out for it in the Morning Post because the Post generally gives the Gazette description of the reasons why it was given. At any rate it is only a question of time until it is given out and I have it sure enough. I am of course very pleased and you have no need to be ashamed of your son. Two other officers in the battalion were given the same medal: Paddison and Johnston by name.

They went out and brought in a wounded man by day time but I am sorry to tell you Johnston is dead, having died of wounds received two days afterwards. However our battalion got more crosses than any in the Division except one which had the same number, three.

Thank you all very much for your letters and parcels. The little torch is excellent and will suit me exceedingly well and the brown bread was a very nice change.

There is one thing I must describe to you and that is the church of a famous village where there has been fighting for nearly two years now. I suppose this place has been shelled as much as anywhere in the war areas: hardly a stone is left on another. The church is as bad as everything else: its walls are only half their original height and everything above them is gone while heaps of stones are piled 10 feet high on the floor. Outside the main entrance is a large crucifix practically untouched. A little has been chipped off the head and right hand and there are a few marks but that is all. Most wonderful of all there is a shell sticking in the base of the cross unexploded: had it exploded the cross would have come to the ground. This is the only thing left in the midst of ruins.

The chateau gardens are still flowering but it is unsafe to try and get any [roses] because a sniper watches the place.

Of course we know no more idea than you when the war will end but I can say this, we have the upper hand in our part of the line. The German never starts anything, he may retaliate and he is always ready to give it up. We can fire I should think three shells to his one here. We have the initiative at any rate and it is very comforting to know our artillery will always support us so well. Of course there was tremendous enthusiasm over the adherence of Romania[13] to our cause and Italy's declaration of war on Germany.[14] This will shorten the war considerably I expect.

Well mother, I must draw to an end: today is Sunday and we had a very good morning service with Communion after, where quite a number communicated including myself. This afternoon I had out my horse and took a ride for exercise. It was my first attempt at a long ride and it has made me pretty stiff but one must learn though it may be painful ...

Please also remember me to all who inquire for me and every other friend. Thank you so much for the Chronicle. It was a great pleasure to be able to hear of old friends through it. It came to me in the trenches. Thanks for all letters and parcels.

B.E.F.
France
[Probably early September 1916]

Dear Dr Norwood

It was a great pleasure to find a letter from you waiting for me at lunch this morning and I was very glad to hear all your news. I knew that you had been appointed to Marlborough and I was intending to congratulate you when I could find time for a letter: however please accept my warmest good wishes for your success when you have to make the change. I saw the news one night in the trenches when a paper was sent up and it came to me almost as a blow because I used to find the visits I paid you when I came on leave one of the greatest pleasures of being home. However I shall take an early opportunity of seeing you when I get the chance. I am sorry to see the school Casualty List mounting up so quickly but it is all in a good cause and one cannot help being proud of friends who have laid down their lives and for oneself one feels almost glad to be in the danger of it. War does bring out the qualities that count: and it is a great moulder of things great and good. I feel now that life is more worth living than ever it was before though at the same time one feels ready to lay it down if one must. The death of Langford was a great shock to me: as I had seen a lot of him and he had always been so friendly and so glad of anything good that came my way. A better fellow I never knew and you must be proud of the fine men that have passed through the school. Perhaps you have heard about his death: but in a way I can tell you more about it almost than anyone else. The division made an attack on the German trenches in a district often attacked before. It was timed to take place on a Sunday but the weather was unfavourable for aircraft and so it was put off until the following Wednesday. The Boche I suppose from his balloons had seen our preparations and collected troops and artillery and shelled our communications trenches and the roads we used behind the lines. On Wednesday we bombarded his trenches for five hours and then attacked. Our brigade had to attack a line of trenches on the right of a very strong salient which the bombardment had not reduced so when the Gloucesters went over about 6 o'clock they were simply mown down in waves by machine gun fire from this salient on that flank. The Brigades on our right and left got in and so did the next division but had to come back later for want of support. Langford was hit in the shoulder but still went on and was hit again. He was brought back about 50 yards and a message was sent in to say he would bleed to death if not rescued but it was impossible to get to him.

Two companies of my battalion had been moved up in support and that night we relieved the Gloucesters. I was told about Langford and was shown the spot where he was supposed to be and informed he was still alive. I went out to search as soon as it was dark and searched nearly all night but unfortunately it was not the right place and though I found several wounded men I could not find him. Next day however we could see an officer about 50 yds from the German wire shouting, blowing his whistle and waving a handkerchief. We could not bring him in by day but as soon as it was dark we got him in though it was a bit risky as we knew the Hun had seen him. I helped as I thought it was Langford as far as I could see. But it was someone else and he told me Langford was dead. I heard later they had been put together in the same shell hole and so I am afraid Langford must have bled to death. This officer slept the first night and so his voice was not there to guide us and he crawled away the next day so that when we found him he was alone.

I shall never forget the sight of those trenches the night we took over. I had four bays allotted to me: in them I found five dead men and two wounded in a dug-out: by the duckboards there were lying more wounded who had been brought in but not removed: the parapet of one bay was breached down to the firing step and next was almost as bad. The traffic trench at the back was choked: all day the dug-outs had been smashed in and the woodwork was smouldering: equipment and stores of all sorts were lying about: and in front of the trench dead and wounded were lying in rows while the whole place reeked of explosive. I did my best to find Jack Langford and had all the holes and ditches searched as far as possible but no trace of him was ever discovered.

I can only tell you of one more distinction for Bristolians and that is for myself. I have just been allotted the Military Cross: the award has not been published a week out here and will be a month at least before it is in the Gazette. However I have to wear the ribbon and I hope some day they will send me home to get the Cross. I am glad to be able to bring a decoration home as my mother and brothers will like it so much and of course it gives me a certain reputation. Am now Lewis Gun Officer of the battalion. It gives me more work in many ways but I like it as it is a fairly responsible and independent command. I have a horse to ride and live at Battalion HQ out here. Of course when in the line I have a lot to do and whatever happens never have to leave the front line trenches. So it requires a good man and I trust I shall prove equal to it if ever we are really tried.

I must now close but I hope leave will start soon and I shall be able to reach Bristol before you go to Marlborough. I congratulate Marlborough on its good fortune but I shall feel it is a big blow to Bristol. However St Johns is a connection that cannot be severed...

P.S. If there are any extracts from this letter relating to Langford you would care to publish in the next Chronicle, please suppress my name.

B.E.F.
[Probably early October 1916]

Dear Mother

We are out of the trenches again and are lucky to be so because the weather is very wet: it started to rain the day we came out and has rained since. Of course it makes it very unpleasant as it is and we find we have not much to do but it must be much worse in the trenches. We were in rather a long time and had it quite fine except for half a day's rain. We had a rather rough time this time: in some ways it was the worst we have had. The enemy opposite us had two trench mortars, both of large size one indeed being the heaviest they had. Well they kept up a fire against us all the time we were in: I mean of course at intervals, sometimes quite long but we never felt we were safe from them as they used to send them over at all hours. The only time I felt really safe was at breakfast time if we had breakfast at 8 o'clock. These trench mortars can send a shell very high up: it does not travel fast and falls very steeply, being meant to fall into the trench and not skim over like the artillery do. As they travel slowly you can see them coming and are able to get away when once you have made up your mind where they are coming ...

We had some fired at us every day, some days more, some days less. They are terribly destructive as the shells are filled with high explosive and they are not meant for man-killing so much as for blowing in trenches. Fortunately they are not very accurate though one or two did actually land right in the trench. I suppose the heavy trench mortar is the most powerful thing one has to meet. In spite of their continual fire, their great power and their good shooting we had no casualties though the escapes were providential. One night indeed we had about a dozen fall where we had twenty men: and they could not be found afterwards. But we organised a search party to dig them out because we thought they must have been buried or blown to pieces: but when we got there we found they had all escaped into the lines of the next battalion and no one was seriously hurt though some had been struck by pieces of falling earth and rubbish.

Otherwise this last time in the trenches was uneventful though we tried hard to capture some prisoners. One prisoner has been captured near us who had only been in the trench 15 minutes: it was his first time in and he had only just come up in a relieving unit. Now he is safe in our hands and will see no more of the war ...

I have had many letters of congratulations, one from Mr Powell of St Johns, another from the Vicar; letters from Bert and Mabel, Auntie Lizzie at Newton Abbot, Mrs Robinson at Brentwood and Mr Sutton. I have also had two letters from Heybridge and a very nice cake: and a letter from Dorothy Robinson at Brentwood as well.

I am enclosing two photographs which may interest, one of myself on my horse and the other the Doctor of the Battalion, an officer named Lawrence attached to us and myself again. I hope you will like them. I have a very good horse now, a big powerful black one though rather slow. He is as you can see a handsome animal and looks very well. He was at one time ridden by Sir John Barnsley but as he landed Sir John's groom into hospital for seven weeks Sir John got rid of him. However he is much quieter now but still is inclined to be wicked. However he gets better all the time and no fault can be really found with him. Of course he takes my weight quite easily as I am not very heavy. I like him very much and shall keep him. I hope you will like the photo: we all three were taken separately but mine has come out best. It took some little time to get into pose and then my groom had to go through all kinds of antics to attract the horse's attention and make him hold his head up and prick his ears up. However we were successful at last.

I am going to send one to Mr Powell as he tells me he has only a photo taken from a Bristol newspaper of me: perhaps you have seen it and know how it came there. At any rate I know some tales of my doings have got into the Worcestershire papers. Such is fame apparently.

I do not know what else there is to tell you except that the nights are very long now and add considerably to our work. In fact they are nearly double the length they were at first and it makes a tour in the trenches much more tiring. Night is the time when everyone is on the alert: day time is the time of rest.

By the way for a day or two I have had charge of a Company but I go back to the Lewis Gun again in a day or two. I am getting to be almost Senior Subaltern now: there are only three above me and two will be captains any day now and maybe I shall be a captain too soon. It all depends on the casualties we have: the subalterns become captains when they have charge of a company for a month. So if there are casualties in the ranks senior to me and I have to take command of a company I become a captain if I hold it for 30 days. That is the system of promotion out here.

I am in good health still: but I shall be glad if you would send my cardigan soon. It has not been cold lately: in fact it has been and still is quite warm but any day it may be cold now. The trees here are not turning colour or dropping their leaves yet, though in Old England they must be doing both I suppose. It is also I should think much warmer here than at home. Well I will close with lots of love to everyone ...

Tell Aunt at home I am very pleased with her letter and want another one pretty quick. I am looking forward to seeing Aunt once more bustling about. I am sure it does me good to see her always so busy. Well especial love to Aunt and Harold and Walt. I am looking forward to a line from Walter and thank Harold for his letter; love above all to yourself and father and the best wishes to everyone

from your loving son Stanley.

P.S. Garrison Duty abroad, please tell Walt, includes the Garrison battalions here in France, who find various duties such as road and traffic police, guards over bridges and stores and all that sort of thing, quite close behind the lines in the shell area.

Stanley

# KILLED IN ACTION

$O$n Saturday 14th October the Booker family in Bristol received a telegram in the late afternoon. It contained the news they must have dreaded. The torn envelope still survives as eloquent testimony to the emotion of those moments. The telegram reads: 'T/5757 Regret to inform you Lieut S C Booker 7th Battn Worcester regt killed in action 11th Oct the Secretary of the State for War expresses his sympathy Colonel in charge territorial force records Warwick.'

In early October, B Company had been ordered to prepare for a raid on the German lines. It took place on Tuesday 10th October. The following account is based on Major Green's recollections. On the night of the 10th, the raiders (about 90 men) met at headquarters at Lansdowne Road which was 200 yards behind the British front line trenches and near the La Bassée Road. Unfortunately the moon was full and when it came out suddenly from behind the clouds, it illuminated the scene as bright as day. The raiders went over the parapet at 10.30 but they could be seen for over 100 yards as they crossed No Man's Land. They were timed to attack at 11 o'clock through a gap made in the German wire by the 18-pounder guns which had been directed that way during the week. At 10.50 an enemy machine gun opened fire from inside the gap and Very lights lit up the raiders. Some time later Sgt Baker of

The telegram envelope delivered on Saturday 14th October, late in the afternoon

the raiding party returned and asked for Major Green. He reported that the men were fired on whenever they attempted to move and asked for artillery fire to protect them so they could escape. This was refused as it would have led to retaliatory fire, making it impossible for the men to cross No Man's Land safely. But the order was given to retire.

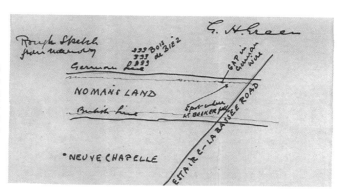

Major Green sent SCB's family this sketch to show where Stanley was killed near the German front line

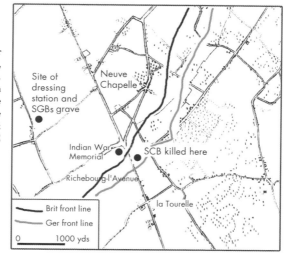

The front line near Neuve Chapelle, October 1916. Based on a map in *The Worcestershire Regiment in the Great War* by Capt H FitzM. Stacke MC

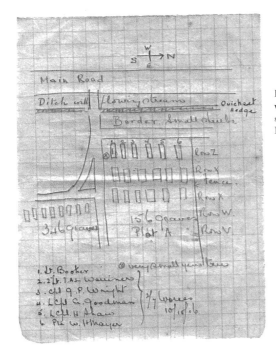

Plan of the cemetery where SCB is buried, sent to his parents by Major Green

Major Green then decided to lead a rescue party across No Man's Land. Stanley volunteered to join him to search for the wounded. They set out and came across a badly wounded man, Sgt Lloyd, 15 yards from the gap in the German wire. They began to pull him backwards along the ground. German machine gun fire hit Lloyd again and broke his arm. They tied his two hands together over his body with a khaki handkerchief to prevent the wounded arm dragging along the ground. They found a disused duckboard and placed him on it to act as a sort of sledge across the mud. At this point the moon came out from behind a cloud and lit up the whole scene. Stanley was shot dead through the head and heart and died immediately.

Unusually, it is possible to indicate with some precision where Stanley died. The War Diary says that the raid was made at 5.11.a.3.2. We know the exact place from trench maps and Major Green later sent the family a sketch indicating the place, about 150 yards east from where the Estaire-La Bassee road crossed the German front line, 400 yards south of the crossroads.

Stanley's body was probably taken by trench tramway to the cemetery by the Advanced Dressing Station at Saint-Vaast. The cemetery itself was in an orchard between farm buildings. A Pioneer Sergeant dug his grave and he was buried on Thursday 12th October, next to 2nd Lt T Warriner. A wooden cross was hurriedly made before the battalion left for the Somme. It bore the words: 'Killed In Action, Rescuing a Comrade'. One of the officers wrote to tell his parents that people from a nearby village had put flowers on his grave and continued to do so for many months. They were perhaps from a farm where he had been billeted.

A puzzling letter was received by the family some time later. It had no address and no signature but simply reported that a group of officers in the regiment believed that Stanley deserved to be recommended for the Victoria Cross. They said he had rescued over twenty-four lives.

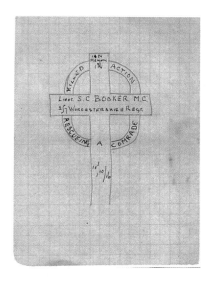

Sketch of the wooden
cross on SCB's grave

The official headstone near the entrance
to the cemetery at St Vaast Post

# TRACKING DOWN THE BOOKERS

The process by which a name was transformed into a real person owes everything to the persistence of several Year 9 pupils who insisted that we should go further than the bare outline in the original folders of library and regimental archive material. There must be relatives still in Bristol... There must be someone still alive who knew the family... Why not use the internet? So we began by writing to all 14 Bookers in the Bristol telephone directory hoping that someone might be related to Stanley. There was no connection with any of them. The school archivist mentioned that Stanley's older brother Harold, born in 1891 had been at Bristol Grammar School but no record of later contact with him survived. A friend who was an expert in family history research gave us the names of several Bookers working on their family histories in other parts of the country and we contacted them. No response. The Rector of St. Bartholomew's Church near the family home in Bristol, knew nothing about the family although street directories showed Mrs Sarah Booker still living in Chesterfield Road until the early 1940s and Stanley's obituary said the family were regular worshippers at the church.

Then a breakthrough. I noticed from the school staff address list that one of my colleagues lived in the house next door to the Booker's old address. Might the person they bought the house from be still alive and have known the Bookers? She asked her husband. Yes, he bought the house from the Burrows family (street directories showed they had been there since 1919) and he knew the address of the Burrows' daughter who still lived in Bristol. Perhaps she could remember something. Yes, but not much because she was a young girl when Mrs Booker moved away from Chesterfield Road. 'I was taken by my father to visit Mrs Booker in her new home. My clearest memory is of going by train from Montpelier Station to the next stop at Stapleton Road and then we walked to a large house in Easton, not too far away. It might have been the Vicarage. After having tea we returned home.'

Optimism soared. Easton is a late-Victorian suburb of terraced houses and large houses are few and far between. It must have been the Vicarage that she remembered and street directories showed that the Vicar from 1939 to the early 1950s was the Rev Walter Booker, perhaps Mrs Booker's nephew or even Stanley's brother. Perhaps the Rev Walter Booker had had children and they would know about family papers. We wrote to all the Bookers in the current Crockford's Directory, thinking that clergymen often produce clergymen sons but all enquiries drew a blank. I then turned to a friend who has an encyclopaedic knowledge of the church in Bristol. He provided the information that a Miss Dorothy Mills remembered Walter Booker in Easton in the 1950s and she suggested we should contact the Rev Bryan Jones who as a young curate had worked with Walter Booker. Mr Jones was a mine of information. He thought that Walter was probably Stanley's brother (he had often talked about a brother killed in the war) and that he had also been at Bristol Grammar School and was a bachelor. When he died in the early 1970s he left some books to Mr Jones who remembered that the executor of his will was a cousin from somewhere in Devon.

The next stage was to locate a copy of the will and discover the names of the Executors. All this time the pupils in Year 9 were following the story with all the attention normally given to *EastEnders*. Next, a visit to the Bristol Probate Office and a search on the microfiche for the exact date of death of the Rev Walter Booker (14th April 1974) and a reference number; then the letter of administration attached to the will was produced within eight minutes. This gave a Bristol solicitor as one executor and John Bosanko of St Luke's College, Exeter as the other. Luckily, an unusual name. Was he still alive and living in Exeter? The telephone directories in the City Library had no Bosanko in Exeter but a J Bosanko in Paignton. The last enquiry ... yes, he was a distant cousin of the three Booker brothers, none of whom had any children. By extraordinary luck Walter Booker had never destroyed any papers that might be useful and John and his sister Mary had boxes of Booker family papers in their attic. It was an extraordinary collection, everything from birth certificates, school prize lists, photographs, enlistment papers to letters home from training and the front, postcards, Stanley's cap badge and the telegram announcing his death, still in its torn envelope. John and Mary Bosanko very generously placed the collection on loan to the school archives and this story based on Stanley's surviving letters to his mother is the result. A name has become a real person.

# ILLUSTRATIONS AND MAPS

page

6   Stanley Booker in 1916. (Bristol Grammar School Archives)

10   SCB with his brothers. (John Bosanko)

12   No. 41 Pembroke Road in 2003. (Graham Fellows)

12   Boyce's Avenue, Clifton in 1913. (J and D Fisher)

13   Dr. Cyril Norwood, Headmaster of Bristol Grammar School. (School Archives)

14   The Great Hall at the school before 1914. (School Archives)

14   The school 1st XV in 1911. (School Archives)

15   Bristol Grammar School before 1914. (MJ Tozer)

16   SCB in 1912. (School Archives)

20   No. 64 Chesterfield Road in 2003. (Graham Fellows)

22   Recruiting at the Colston Hall. (Andrew Palmer)

23   The International Exhibition at Ashton Gate. (MJ Tozer)

23   Taking bedding into one of the buildings. (MJ Tozer)

23   D Company being fed. (MJ Tozer)

24   Drilling at Ashton Gate. (MJ Tozer)

24   Digging trenches at Ashton Gate. (MJ Tozer)

24   A church parade outside Ashton Gate Brewery. (MJ Tozer)

28   Heybridge Hall. (The Maldon Society Archives)

31   St. Peter's Tower, Maldon. (The Maldon Society Archives)

38   The wedding at Heybridge Hall. (Derek Maldon Fitch)

41   A Worcestershire Territorial company at Maldon, Essex. (© The Worcestershire and Sherwood Foresters Regiment, WFR)

41   Returning from a route march. (© WFR Archives)

72   Trench catapult with obstacles in background. (© WFR Archives)

84   Bayonet practice at Brentwood in 1915. (© WFR Archives)

85   Candahar Barracks, Tidworth, c1912. (Terry Crawford)

92   Officers of the 2/7th Battalion, the Worcestershire Regiment. (© WFR Archives)

95 Using a box periscope in a training trench. (© WFR Archives)

114 SCB on horseback in France 1916. (School Archives)

116 Worcestershire Territorials in typical French farm. (© WFR Archives)

119 Worcestershire Territorials resting en route for the front.
(© WFR Archives)

126 The telegram envelope. (School Archives)

127 Sketch of the place where SCB died. (School Archives)

128 Plan of the cemetery at Richebourg-St-Vaast. (School Archives)

129 Sketch of the wooden cross on SCB's grave. (School Archives)

130 SCB's headstone in the cemetery. (School Archives)

143 The memorial in the Great Hall at BGS. (Stephen Morris)

## MAPS

100 Part of the Western Front in 1916

127 The front line at Neuve–Chapelle

# NOTES

## School Days

1. **Cyril Norwood**:1875-1956, scholar of St John's College, Oxford; Headmaster of BGS (1906-16) then of Marlborough and Harrow; President of St John's College, Oxford. He wrote the Norwood Report which recommended secondary education for all children; it was passed into legislation by his old Marlborough pupil, RA Butler. Knighted 1938.

2. **battels**: Charges at Oxford and Cambridge colleges for board and lodging, paid termly at this time. On this occasion they totalled £16.12.6d and included £1.8.0d for bedmaker and 5.0d for Use of Baths but nothing on wine. Other expenses such as Tutorage brought the total to £33.8.6d of which £25 was paid by the Scholarship, leaving SCB to find £8.8.6d. (Approximately £422 by today's values.) Under the old money system one pound was divided into 20 shillings and each shilling contained 12 pence. The decimal system began in 1971.

3. **Mr and Mrs Ball**: Sidney Ball was Fellow and Tutor in classics at St John's College for 36 years; he wrote *Socialism and Individualism* and died in 1918.

4. **the Gaisford**: A prestigious prize awarded annually at Oxford University for writing Greek verse or Greek prose, worth £21 at this time.

## Joining Up: No 14605

1. **The Lord Mayor**: Alderman John Swaish; he was away on holiday at Llandrindod Wells when war was declared but returned on 7th August.

2. **Col Burgess and Capt Blennerhasset**: Burgess came from Yate and joined the South Gloucestershire Militia in 1880. He was a popular commander of the 12th Battalion. Blennerhasset had seen service in the Matabele War and in the Boer War (1899-1902). He was at the Siege of Ladysmith.

3. **White City**: The exhibition opened in Ashton Meadows in June but closed in August owing to the cancellation of many excursion trains. The name White City was presumably borrowed from the London exhibition of that name held in 1908. The War Office bought the site to turn into accommodation and a parade ground for Bristol's Own.

4. **Sir Hugh Stewart**: 1858-1942, educated at Wellington and Sandhurst, he was the 4th baronet. He was the Brigadier-General commanding 77th Brigade from 1914 to 1915. He served in the Boer War.

## Training with the Worcestershire Regiment

1. **Heybridge Hall**: Home of the Stebbing family, the thirteenth-century building fell into disrepair and was destroyed by fire in 1997. It was subsequently demolished.

2. **square tower**: Known as St Peter's tower, at the corner of High Street and Market Hill. The nave collapsed in the late seventeenth century and part of the tower is now the Maeldune Heritage Centre.

3. **Mr and Mrs Stebbing**: A family of wealthy farmers and cattle dealers; they left Heybridge Hall in 1923. They had five children who enjoyed playing practical jokes on the soldiers.

4. **the wedding**: 11th May 1915 between the eldest daughter, Ethel Julia, and Capt Thomas Maldon Fitch.

5. **Todd's**: Matthew Todd, Civil and Military Tailors at 31 College Green, Bristol. They advertised that they could supply Officers Service Outfits, Breeches and All Military Equipment at shortest notice.

6. *The Times*: The report says that a Zeppelin was sighted shortly before midnight, came up the Blackwater, circled the Tower and dropped seven bombs on Heybridge. It continued: "The Maldon police have received no report of any personal injuries but an old hen was killed."

7. **Thomas Maldon Fitch**: He was gassed at the Battle of Loos in September 1915 and died in 1931. The family were prominent in Maldon for many generations.

8. **Lord Salisbury**: 4th Marquess, 1861-1947, son of the prime minister. He fought in the Boer War, became a Major General and commanded the 2nd South Midland Division, later renamed the 61st Division, until the end of 1915. He held many political offices, 1900-29.

9. **Sir John Barnsley**: 1858-1926, he played a prominent part in public life in Birmingham. He was later a Brigadier General; known as a strong Methodist.

10. **Lord Deerhurst**: 1865-1928, of Croome Court, Worcestershire. He was a colonel in the Territorial Force Reserve. He predeceased his father the 9th Earl of Coventry so never succeeded to the title.

11. **Walter**: 1894-1974, Stanley's younger brother who was also at BGS. He became a clergyman and preserved meticulously the family papers on which this book is based.

12. **take a hand**: a recurring theme is Stanley's concern about his brothers' role in the war effort; neither served in the armed forces and in the case of Walter this may have been partly due to lack of height (he was 5ft 3 inches) and poor eyesight. By May 1915 voluntary recruitment was not thought to be producing enough men and there were rumours that a national register of all men of military age would be compiled as a prelude to conscription.

13. **Boreham Park**: North of Chelmsford, about 10 miles from Maldon; the seventeenth-century hall was surrounded by a park containing red deer.

14. **Jack Langford**: William John Langford, a contemporary and close friend of SCB at BGS; they were in the 1st XV together in 1910; a lieutenant in the 6th Gloucesters, he was killed in action in July 1916. SCB describes the search for him in his letter to Dr Norwood of early September 1916. His father was a jeweller and goldsmith with premises at 30 College Green. They installed one of the first electric clocks in Bristol and it can still be seen outside the shop with the words Langford's Electric on the face.

15. **Home Service men**: Soldiers who had not volunteered to serve overseas and were therefore used as second line units for Home Defence.

16. **Harold**: 1891-197?, Stanley's older brother who was also at BGS. He may have worked in munitions during the war and later became an engineer; the only brother to marry but there were no children.

17. **conscription**: The Military Service Act of January 1916 required that all unmarried men aged 18 to 41 would be liable to be called up unless they were in a reserved occupation; however this was deemed to be unfair and the Act of June 1916 declared all men, single or married, liable to be called up.

18. **Mr Powell**: 1865-1935, Fellow and Tutor in Classics at St John's College for 45 years; he wrote *New Chapters in the History of Greek Literature*.

19. **inoculated**: Against typhoid; the British pathologist Almroth Wright is usually given the credit for developing the first typhoid vaccination in 1896 but Richard Pfeiffer, a German bacteriologist claimed that he was the first. The credit should perhaps be shared.

20. **thoroughly disorganised**: The whole division had a poor reputation; it was not equipped adequately or trained consistently; in addition, the officers were changed frequently.

21. **eyesight**: The whole family suffered from poor eyesight; SCB was unable to pass the test at the recruiting station in 1914 without the help of glasses and this was blamed for his failure to be commissioned at that time.

22. **Kitchener**: Herbert Horatio,1850-1916, the face on the famous poster; also soldier and statesman who served in Egypt, the Sudan, India and South Africa. He was Secretary of State for War 1914-1916 and the first to realise a huge army was needed. He was drowned on 5th June 1916 when HMS Hampshire was sunk off Orkney by a German mine when he was en route to a conference in Russia.

23. **Sir Daniel Gooch**: 1816-1889, railway pioneer and inventor; for 27 years he was locomotive superintendent of the GWR. Hylands Park is south west of Chelmsford.

24. **the *Chronicle***: The Bristol Grammar School magazine, produced three times a year at this time.


## From Bisley to Brentwood

1. **conscription**: another rumour; it did not begin until January 1916 although it was a major issue in the autumn of 1915, with some ministers threatening to resign if it was not brought in. The demand for conscription arose more from anger against 'slackers' than for the need for more men. The army had more men that it could equip and train. Conscription eventually produced only 40,000 men per month, less than half the number who had enlisted voluntarily.

2. **Sir George Marks**: 1858-1938, M.P. for North Cornwall; an engineer and patent expert.

3. **the munitions question**: Presumably the shortage of shells and ammunition and the frequent complaints that a high proportion of shells did not explode because the fuses had not been set properly in the factories. David Lloyd George became the first Minister of Munitions in May 1915 and set about solving the problems with typical energy.

4. **dirigible**: The French version of the Zeppelin; it means literally a balloon that can be steered.

5. **victories in France**: This was the Franco-British autumn offensive launched in the last week of September 1915. The papers had got it wrong: the allies could not follow through their attacks. At the Battle of Loos one German division held six British. The Allies lost twice as many men as the Germans.

6. **La Bassée**: South of Neuve-Chapelle and north of Lens near the place where SCB was serving when he was killed.

7. **Invermay**: In Highlands Avenue; demolished in the 1960s and now the site of a block of flats.

8. **Kitchener resigned**: Reported in the papers on 6th November but later denied; there was growing tension between Kitchener and his cabinet colleagues but the public admired him above all other war leaders.

9. **New Clifton**: The Westbury Park suburb of Bristol built in the fields beyond Redland in the

early twentieth-century. The use of this name was an early example of estate agents' licence.

10. **Robertson**: He made a mistake; Kelly's Street Directories give the name as Robinson.

11. **Highwood Schools**: Attached to the Highwood Hospital founded by the London Metropolitan Asylums Board in 1904 to treat children suffering from ophthalmia.

12. **Warley Barracks**: For the Essex Regiment, closed in 1959 but the chapel remains; much of the site is now Ford's European Central Office built in 1964.

13. **canvass**: Presumably refers to Lord Derby's scheme whereby each man of military age had to "attest" that he would serve his country when called to do so.

14. **Vickers Light Gun**: Hiram Maxim invented one of the first machine guns in 1884; this version was produced by the Vickers Company and widely used.

15. **Bailleul**: Typical of the stories circulating about the deviousness of the French.

16. **Walter's birthday**: 18th November.

17. **All Saints, Clifton**: One of the "highest" churches in Bristol; built by G.E. Street in 1864 with the aim of allowing all the congregation to have an unbroken view of chancel, altar and pulpit and participate in the elaborate ritual of services; gutted 1940 and subsequently rebuilt.

18. **windmills**: They have now gone and the nearest restored windmill is at Mountnessing to the north of Brentwood.

19. **Defence of the Realm Act**: Enacted in August 1914 and known as DORA; provided the authority for all kinds of censorship and wartime restriction.

20. **Filton**: A suburb in the north of Bristol where Sir George White and his son founded the British and Colonial Aeroplane Company in 1910. The first military planes in Britain were built at Filton. No. 5065 was built to a French design but not made in Bristol.

21. **Warley**: Probably Christ Church near the barracks, a walk of about two miles.

22. **Lord Petre**: A prominent Roman Catholic family who lived at nearby Thorndon Hall until it was burnt in 1878 and then at Ingatestone Hall. They built many catholic churches in the district.

23. **London defences**: Presumably preparations to protect London by holding back the German invasion in Essex.

24. **reserve**: The list of men who had pledged to serve their country when needed; only half the single men and less than half the married men put their names forward.

25. **White Hart Hotel**: A famous coaching inn dating dating from the fifteenth century with courtyard galleries giving access to rooms on the first floor. It is no longer a hotel but still serves drinks.

26. **Sir John French**: 1852-1925, he served as first commander of the British Expeditionary Force in France 1914-1915; he did not establish good relations with his French allies and had no solution to the stalemate of the trenches, dismissed in December 1915.

27. **Indian Civil Service**: The small number of intellectually gifted British men (and later Indians) who ruled the vast continent of India. They were recruited mainly from Oxford and Cambridge universities and entered the Service by competitive exam, begun in 1853; many were Classics scholars so SCB would have been in good company.

28. **Mr and Mrs Asquith**: He was Prime Minister from 1908-1916 and married Margot Tennant as his second wife in 1894. She was famous for her vivacity and wit, e.g. she was annoyed that the actress Jean Harlow persistently mispronounced her name. When she met her, Margot said, "the t is silent as in Harlow".

29. **recruits**: Presumably the men called up in December 1915 after they had pledged their willingness to serve when needed.

30. **Kinnersley**: The family dentist at 108 Redland Road, Bristol.

31. **money**: There was obviously a concern in the family that Stanley should not fall into debt; when he died in 1916 his estate amounted to £199-1-5d and no debts.

32. **Compulsion Bill**: The Military Service Bill of January 1916 whereby all unmarried men between 18 and 41 were deemed to be in the Army Reserve and liable to be called up unless they were in a "reserved occupation".

33. **Lucy Skinner**: It has not been possible to trace any of the Skinner family; Stanley's mother Sarah was the daughter of Henry Skinner, a butcher of Chilton Road, Bath. She married James Booker in 1889. No photograph of Stanley's parents has been found.

34. **Perham Down**: A mile east of Tidworth on Salisbury Plain, purchased by the War Department in 1897 and used for summer camps by Volunteer battalions; described by some as "an undulating expanse of grass-covered common from which magnificent views can be obtained" and by others as "Perishing Down".

## Salisbury Plain at Last

1. **Candahar Barracks**: Named after the British victory near Candahar in May 1842 . Major-General Sir William Nott's army defeated 8,000 Afghans. By 1880 when Lord Roberts defeated the Afghans besieging the city the name was spelt with a K. The earlier victory was celebrated in the barracks, hence the old spelling.

2. **quinine**: A traditional remedy for a variety of ailments, widely used in India. Kipling describes how he took "quinine in the sherry" at the fort in Lahore.

3. **great gale**: *The Times* reported that over 20,000 trees fell during the storm within a 20 mile radius of Hitchin (also the first swallows were seen near Tiverton).

4. **Bulford Fields:** To the north of the barracks and frequently used for large parades; the tradition was that a regiment paraded there a week or two before going overseas so some men regarded the place with dread and others with eager anticipation.

5. **The King**: George V was assiduous in reviewing parades and took the salute at Bulford Fields on at least 11 occasions during the Great War.

6. **Wherwell Park**: The Priory was the residence of Colonel Atherton Jenkins and it was surrounded by parkland.

7. **Amport Park**: Belonged to the Marquess of Winchester; a mansion built in 1887 standing in a park of 200 acres.

8. **Ludgershall**: A station near Tidworth on the Midland and South Western Junction Railway, linking Cheltenham with Southampton; the war made it the busiest station on the system.

# At the Front

1. **busy**: On 6th June A Company relieved D Company in the Right Sector, Ferme du Bois and remained there until 9th June when they were relieved by the 2/6th Gloucesters.

2. **this naval battle**: The Battle of Jutland began on 31st May between the British and German navies; it was the only major naval battle during the war. Both sides claimed to have won. The British lost 14 ships and 6,000 sailors; the Germans 13 and 2,500 sailors but the German fleet did not leave its base at Kiel again for the rest of the war.

3. **famous village**: Vieille Chapelle where the battalion was stationed at this time.

4. **a raid**: Probably as described in the War Diary: "Heavy bombardment of Enemy Line 10.55pm. 1 Company and 3 machine guns entered German trenches ... did considerable damage with bombs to Germans in trenches and dugouts. The party left the German lines at 11.20pm and were all back at 11.30pm."

5. **aeroplanes**: They were first used for reconnaissance but by the end of 1914 airmen were firing at one another with revolvers and rifles. The first fighter planes appeared in 1915 and were equipped with machine guns. By 1918 the Royal Flying Corps had 22,171 aircraft.

6. **big push**: Presumably refers to the Battle of the Somme which began on 1st July 1916.

7. **Webb**: JP Webb is sitting next to Stanley in the 1st XV photograph of 1911. He was also killed.

8. **out of the trenches again**: They had been in for seven days and duties consisted of repairing parapets, collecting the wounded and dead from No Man's Land, re-wiring the front, collecting salvage and burying the dead.

9. **an attack**: This must refer to the disastrous attack at Fromelles, launched on 19th July. The aim was to deter the Germans from moving men and guns to the Somme. The start of battle was postponed for two days because of mist and this gave the Germans plenty of time to prepare. One participant said it was more a massacre than a battle. Stanley won his M.C. rescuing wounded men in the aftermath.

10. **out of range**: In Laventie.

11. **fall back**: The Australians felt a sense of betrayal that they had not been better supported. They lost 5,533 men.

12. *Gazette*: It appeared on 22nd September 1916.

13. **adherence of Romania**: Neutral at the outbreak of war, Romania was promised by the allies certain regions such as Transylvania, at the end of the war, and she declared war on Austria-Hungary on 27th August 1916.

14. **Italy's declaration**: Although Italy had joined the allies and declared war on Austria in May 1915 she did not declare war on Germany until August 1916.

## ACKNOWLEDGEMENTS

Many people have been very generous with time and advice and I would like to thank them all: Lawrence Aspden, Curator of Special Collections at Sheffield University Library, Nick Attwood, Anne Bradley, archivist at Bristol Grammar School, Angela Brassley, Janet Brewer, John and Mary Bullock, Faye Catterall, Terry Crawford, Kirsty Davies-Walters, Margaret Day, Graham Fellows, Derek Fitch, Brian and Melanie Guy, Pat Hase, Pete John who found Stanley Booker's Service file in the Public Record Office, the Rev Bryan Jones, Maggie Lane, Martin Lee, Helen Littlejones, Richard Maidment, Neil Matthews, Dr Roger Pritchard who kindly shared his great knowledge of recruitment in 1914, Michael Riordan, Assistant Archivist of St John's College, Oxford, Liam Robinson, Daniel and Katie Ronald, John Sansom who has been the most understanding of publishers, Mike Tozer, Dr. Jennifer Ward, Patrick Weaver, Michael Whitfield, Andy Williamson and my colleagues in the History Department at BGS.

John and Mary Bosanko who own the letters have played an invaluable role by their encouragement and enthusiasm. Without their kindness this book would not have been possible. Lt Col CP Love, Honorary Archivist of the Worcestershire Regiment, has been endlessly patient in answering the sort of questions that only someone who doesn't know a bangalore from a bayonet would need to ask. My wife and family have been very kind and generous in accepting the presence of Stanley Booker as a member of the family during the last few months. I am very grateful.

Barry Williamson
April 2003